This book is dedicated to everyone we have had the honour of sharing a meal with, our lives are richer because of who we spend our time with. May we make our world a little more kind and peaceful by the way we eat.

A JULIE GIBBS BOOK

for

SIMON & SCHUSTER
AUSTRALIA
A GIBBS COMPANY

GEMMA DAVIS & TRACY NOELLE

THE
COMPASSIONATE
KITCHEN

A plant-based cookbook

WHY PLANTS?

There are many paths that may lead us to choosing to eat more plants and less meat. It could be health reasons, since plants are high in live enzymes, are alkalising and full of antioxidants and fibre. It might be driven by the environmental impact of animal agriculture. Many studies, including those by the United Nations, have concluded it is causing major impacts such as deforestation, water pollution and greenhouse gas emissions. Plus, animal agriculture is one of the largest land and fresh water users in a world that is not getting any bigger, with a population that is not getting any smaller.

Perhaps swapping meat for plants is being driven by the desire to not harm animals, especially since we know we can live a healthy life without eating them.

Or maybe you have ended up with a plant-based cookbook because the time has come and you know that veggie meals can be complete and delicious as a stand alone. Simple as that.

Whatever your path, eating this way can be creative, tasty and filling, and we hope this book makes eating a plant-based diet, whether for a meal or for life, enjoyable – and easy! It allows you to experience tweaked classics as well as a range of new combinations that we had lots of fun coming up with. We believe we can shape our health, our lives and communities by what we choose to eat, and it's so much better if it tastes great while we do it!

HEALTH TIPS

This may not be a health book, but most of the recipes within these pages have the bonus of being good for you. Food plays such a large part in how we feel physically and emotionally, so the more accessible and tasty the meals are, the better it is for us personally, for our families and communities. Plus, the better we feel, the more likely we are to keep eating well!

Here are a few naturopathic tips that can help get you started on the road to feeling great. Keep in mind that leaving out or cutting down on artificial flavours and colours, sugars, processed foods, caffeine and alcohol goes a long way and leaves more room for the good stuff!

GOOD FATS

You do not need to fear fats. Fats are needed in our body to create hormones, improve brain function, nourish our hair, skin and nails and much, much more. The myth that fat makes you fat has been busted – to maintain a healthy weight, good fats are our friend as they help with metabolism and feeling satiated after eating. The key is knowing which fats to consume and how to consume them, because not all fats are created equal.

It is best to avoid products that contain trans-fats which are are linked to many health issues. These are altered unsaturated fats, typically created through the processing of vegetable oils through hydrogenation, and found in many baked or processed products at the supermarket. It is also worth cooking with oils that are relatively stable at high temperatures, such as coconut oil, extra virgin olive oil or even macadamia nut oil, and decreasing your use of vegetable oils. Using flaxseed oil on your salads is also a great way to get more omega-3 in your diet. Eat those avocados, pre-soaked nuts and seeds and even include algae oil, either in supplements or you can put the oil in smoothies.

WATER

Drink more water. One of the easiest and cheapest ways to get glowing skin is to drink 2 litres of filtered water a day. You may think if you drink more liquid you will be puffy, but the opposite is true when it comes to water – it will help flush impurities out of your system and keep you hydrated and supple. Our bodies are made of about 60% water, so it simply makes sense. Make sure the water you drink is filtered, and whenever you can, try not to drink it from plastic bottle – they are an environmental nightmare and can leach small amounts of chemicals into the water.

SLEEP (or even better, meditation)

Sleep is oh-so-important to allow the body time to rest and rejuvenate and studies show 7–9 hours is the optimal amount. While we are sleeping, our skin makes new collagen and the body boosts blood flow, both part of the repair process that helps reduces wrinkles and dryness. Add to good sleep by meditating daily, and gain an even more extraordinarily deep state of rest – several times deeper than sleep. This is why those who meditate tend to not only seem calmer, they look more refreshed too.

WHOLE FOODS

This is a really basic concept but one that if followed, can change your diet and overall health dramatically. Remember, less out of a packet and more out of the ground; the nearer the food is to its natural state, the better. We don't want to overload our bodies with toxins, and when we eat highly processed foods, this is what happens. We can cause inflammation in our system that can result in acne, cellulite and a dullness in our energy and skin tone.

Whole foods are full of vitamins, minerals and active enzymes that work synergistically, as nature made them. While supplementing with particular foods can be useful, the basic building blocks begin with what we are eating, and nothing can replicate the intricate balance of food as it is grown in the earth.

GUT HEALTH

You can eat all the right things, but if your digestive system is not working optimally, you won't reap the benefits. Bloating, gas, cramps and loose or hard-to-pass stools can all indicate something is not quite right with your gut health and you may not be utilising your nutrients as well as possible. Rashes, headaches, mood swings and a plethora of other issues can also stem from digestive imbalances because the gut is not just digesting food, it is also where much of our immune system lies, where some of our neurotransmitters are made and where much of our detoxification happens.

A naturopath can help you with a more personal diet and herbal protocol but you can also help your gut by including fermented foods, such as kimchi, sauerkraut, miso and coconut yoghurts as well as supplementing with probiotics in your diet. Fermented foods help rebalance the bacteria that colonise our digestive system, providing us with a broad-spectrum of natural bacterias we need to encourage good gut health.

MAKE WHAT YOU EAT COUNT

These days we have a profound dependence on refined, packaged, nutrient-void foods that are full of empty calories, especially from drinks. By consuming these types of foods and drinks, we are filling up on things that don't nourish us rather than foods that do. To spell it out, if you eat a slice of cake for morning tea, you probably won't feel like eating a plate of fruit or if you eat a big bowl of sugary cereal for breakfast you have missed an opportunity to have a plate of vegetables and beans.

ATTITUDE

There is nothing uglier than a bad attitude. It can affect your posture, your aura and, just as our physical health can affect our moods, our emotions can also affect our bodies; from your posture to your digestive system (and we just mentioned how important that is!)

Being authentic, not sweating the small stuff and being kind to yourself and to others goes a long way to living a healthy life.

START
THE DAY
RIGHT

START THE DAY RIGHT

Breakfast is your chance every morning to set the vibe for the day ahead. It doesn't matter what happened yesterday or last week – what will you choose to feed yourself and your family this morning? How will you start *this* day?

The crazy rush hour before school and work squeezes our breakfast time, and for convenience more and more people are relying on food from packages for the first thing they put inside their mouths. These are more often than not highly processed, empty carbs that are high in sugars and even artificial flavours and colours. This isn't what our bodies are yearning for.

It is possible to have fast, high-energy meals that also pack a punch of nutrients, proteins and fats to our carbs, providing us with fuel and sustained energy for longer. This is especially important for the little people to enable their growing bodies and minds to thrive throughout the day. These recipes provide quick and easy options but are still healthy. For breakfast, and throughout the day, we want to have less out of a packet and more out of the ground.

MORNING TIP: Before eating anything, try starting the day with a glass of filtered water with either a squeeze of fresh lemon juice or a dash of apple cider vinegar, to stimulate your digestive system after its rest overnight.

Kale, Kimchi and Avo Bowl

This is a super bowl, one that is packed full of nutrients and makes a naturopath smile.
With the combination of micronutrients from the nori, the probiotics from the fermented vegetables
and miso, the good oil from the coconut, protein from the mushrooms plus a good dose of greens,
it really keeps you energised when you have a big day ahead.

SERVES 1

1 tablespoon miso paste
1 cup porcini or shiitake mushrooms, sliced
2 cups kale, stalks removed and roughly torn
½ cup shredded brussels sprouts
2 teaspoons coconut oil
½ avocado, sliced or scooped
2 tablespoons kimchi or fermented vegetables
   (purchased or see page 141)
1 teaspoon nori flakes
1 teaspoon sesame seeds

Option
1 slice of toasted organic bread.

Combine the miso and mushrooms in a medium
bowl and set aside for 1 minute.

Place the kale, shredded sprouts and coconut
oil in a large bowl and, using your hands,
massage the oil thoroughly into the leaves.

Place a deep frying pan over medium heat.
Add the kale mixture to one side of the pan,
place the mushrooms on the other side and cook
for 3–5 minutes or until soft, stirring frequently.

Serve with avocado and kimchi or fermented
veggies, with nori flakes and sesame seeds
sprinkled over the top.

Toasted Ginger Granola with Poached Pears

The combination of vanilla, poached pears and pops of sweet ginger in this breakfast is extremely warming and comforting and a real winner with children. Most packaged granolas and cereals get their very high levels of sweetness by adding massive amounts of sugar – often the second ingredient. Using a real maple syrup is an unprocessed and much gentler sweetener for our bodies to work with. If you are doing a detox you can always use less maple syrup and leave out the crystallised ginger.

SERVES 4

coconut milk, to serve*

Granola
2 cups rolled oats
½ cup pumpkin seeds
1 cup coconut flakes
⅓ cup maple syrup
2 tablespoons coconut oil, melted
2 teaspoons vanilla extract
2 teaspoons ground cinnamon
1 tablespoon ground turmeric
1 teaspoon ground ginger
2 star anise
juice of 1 orange
½ cup crystallised ginger, cut into small dice

Poached pears
2 cups water
1 tablespoon maple syrup
1 teaspoon vanilla extract
2 pears, peeled, cored and halved or quartered

To make the granola, preheat the oven to 160°C. Line a baking tray with baking paper.

Combine all the ingredients in a large bowl. Spoon onto the prepared tray and bake for 35 minutes, stirring occasionally, taking care not to let it burn.

Remove from the oven and allow to cool. If you are not using it immediately, store the granola in an airtight container.

To prepare the pears, combine the water, maple syrup and vanilla in a medium saucepan and bring to the boil over medium heat. Add the pears and reduce the heat to low. Cover and simmer for 20 minutes or until tender.

Remove the pears from the liquid.

To serve, divide the granola evenly among 4 bowls, top with the pears and drizzle with coconut milk.

Coconut milks have improved greatly recently. The texture is creamy but the flavour isn't overwhelming or mucus producing, as dairy and soy milks can be for many people.

Mango with Coconut Yoghurt and Buckwheat Crumble

No longer do we only have the option of dairy yoghurts or highly processed soy yoghurts to get a wonderful dose of gut-loving probiotics and mouthfuls of wonderful smooth cream. Coconut yoghurt is incredibly easy to make and is a great ingredient to have in your fridge for snacks after school too.

SERVES 4

2 mangoes, sliced
handful of mint leaves (optional)

Coconut Yoghurt
THIS NEEDS TO BE MADE THE NIGHT BEFORE.
1 × 400 ml can coconut cream
2 teaspoons arrowroot
1 probiotic capsule

Buckwheat Crumble
½ cup buckwheat flour
1 cup buckwheat kernels
3 tablespoons coconut oil, melted
½ cup maple syrup
1 teaspoon ground cinnamon
½ teaspoon cardamom pods, roughly
  crushed with back of a spoon

To prepare the yoghurt, preheat the oven to 35°C.

Place the coconut cream and arrowroot in a deep ovenproof saucepan over low heat and cook, whisking, for 3 minutes. Set aside to cool.

Once the cream is cool, add the contents of the probiotic capsule and stir to combine. Cover the saucepan with a lid and place in the oven for 8 hours or overnight.

Transfer the coconut yoghurt to a sterilised jar with a lid and place in the fridge to chill.

To prepare the crumble, preheat the oven to 200°C. Line a baking tray with baking paper.

Combine the crumble ingredients in a large bowl, then spoon onto the prepared tray and bake for 10 minutes. Set aside to cool.

To serve, divide the mango among 4 bowls and top with coconut yoghurt and crumble. Garnish with fresh mint leaves (if using).

Note
You can experiment by adding different flavours to the yoghurt mix, such as vanilla, blueberry etc.

Acai Blood-building Bowl

There are entire Instagram accounts dedicated to the smoothie bowl. Using beets in a bowl like this is a perfect way to get this blood-boosting vegetable into our diet to increase the blood's capacity for carrying oxygen and nutrients.

The high-protein seed mix will make more than you need for this recipe. Store the rest in an airtight container – it's a great thing to have on hand.

SERVES 1

mint leaves, to serve

Toasted Seed Mix
1 cup flaxseeds (linseeds)
1 cup sunflower seeds
1 cup buckwheat kernels
1 cup almonds, sliced or chopped
2 teaspoons ground cinnamon

Smoothie Bowl
100 g frozen acai (unsweetened)
1 beetroot, peeled and chopped
1 cup baby spinach leaves
1 cup frozen mixed berries
½ cup mint leaves
1 serving protein powder
2 medjool dates or prunes

To Serve
To make the toasted seed mix, preheat the oven to 160°C. Line a baking tray with baking paper.

Combine all the ingredients in a large bowl and spoon onto the prepared tray. Bake for 15 minutes, stirring halfway through, then remove from the oven and set aside to cool.

For the smoothie bowl, place all the ingredients in a blender and blend for 3–4 minutes or until smooth. You may need to add a few tablespoons of water to achieve a smooth consistency.

Pour the smoothie mixture into a bowl. Top with a generous sprinkling of toasted seed mix and some fresh mint.

* We prefer to use a fermented rice, pea or hemp protein powder.

Sweet Potato, Mint and Pea Fritters

These fritters are a great way to start your day. Because both sweet potato and peas are high in B6, Vitamin C and Beta-carotene, they boost your immune system and support your blood-sugar levels, rather than giving you spikes in energy. To save time in the morning rush, cook the sweet potato the night before and store it in the fridge, ready to go.

SERVES 4

small handful mint leaves, roughly chopped

Fritters
1 kg sweet potato (about 2 medium), skin on
2 cups peas, fresh or frozen
1 bunch mint, roughly chopped
3 spring onions, chopped
3 tablespoons coconut cream (it's better if you keep the can in the fridge for a few hours before and then you can scoop the creamy part off the top when you are ready to make the fritters)
½ teaspoon salt
⅓ cup almond meal, plus extra if needed
coconut oil, for frying

Hazelnut Mix
½ cup roasted hazelnuts, chopped
½ cup fried shallots

Preheat the oven to 190°C. Place the sweet potatoes on a baking tray and bake for 1 hour or until tender. Cool slightly, then remove the skin. Place the sweet potato flesh in a large bowl and roughly mash.

Meanwhile place the peas in a small saucepan with enough water to just cover and cook for 4–5 minutes or until soft. Drain.

Place the peas, mint, spring onion, coconut cream and salt in a blender or food processor and blend to a course paste – you don't want it to be too smooth.

Add the pea mixture and almond meal to the sweet potato and mix to combine. If the mixture seems a little soft, add a bit more almond meal.

Heat the coconut oil in a frying pan. Spoon ½ cup of the mixture into the pan and flatten slightly. Fry for 3–4 minutes on each side or until well coloured. Depending on the size of your pan, you may need to do this in batches.

Meanwhile, combine the hazelnut mix ingredients in a small bowl.

To serve place 2 fritters on each plate and sprinkle the hazelnut mix and mint over the top.

These also taste great on a bed of greens, such as baby spinach or rocket.

Asian Baked Breakfast Beans

An Australian breakfast staple, Asian style! Serve with avocado, some greens and maybe some sesame seeds on a thick slice of crunchy toast. This recipe can be easily doubled or tripled. Make a big batch for Sunday brunch and savour the leftovers throughout the week.

SERVES 2

1 × 400 g can cannellini beans, drained and rinsed (or 400 g cooked cannellini or Great Northern beans)*

1 teaspoon salted black beans, mashed (available from Asian supermarkets)

½ teaspoon onion powder

2 tablespoons chopped coriander

1 garlic clove, crushed

2 cm piece of ginger, grated

1½ teaspoons tamari

3 tablespoons chilli sauce (purchased or see page 109)

2 slices toast of choice

1 avocado, sliced

1 cup baby spinach leaves

Preheat the oven to 200°C.

Combine the beans, salted black beans, onion powder, coriander, garlic, ginger, tamari and chilli sauce in an ovenproof dish. Cover with foil and bake for 20 minutes or until hot and bubbling.

Serve on toast with avocado and baby spinach.

If using canned beans you can save the brine to use in the aquafaba recipes in the dessert section of this book.

Zucchini Muffins

While muffins are not a substitute for a well-rounded breakfast, with the addition of some nut meals and vegetables they can be a perfect mid-morning pick-me-up. Don't all children hate zucchini? This recipe is the perfect way to hide the dreaded vegetable in a much-loved snack, ready to throw into school lunchboxes for morning tea – and for you to enjoy too.

MAKES 8

¾ cup coconut milk
½ cup coconut oil, melted
½ cup maple syrup
1 cup spelt flour
1 tablespoon baking powder
pinch of salt
¾ cup almond meal
1 cup grated zucchini

Preheat the oven to 180°C and grease 8 holes of a ⅓ cup capacity muffin tin.

Place the coconut milk, coconut oil and maple syrup in a medium bowl and whisk together.

Combine the flour, baking powder, salt, almond meal and zucchini in a separate larger bowl. Add the liquid ingredients and whisk to combine.

Spoon the mixture evenly into the prepared muffin holes, then bake for 25–30 minutes or until firm and lightly coloured.

Super Smoothies

Great for when you are in a rush in the morning instead of just trying to survive on caffeine, or for an afternoon pick-me up, the super smoothie can be put in a jar and taken with you. These recipes have been tried and tested on many little ones for after school or 'second' breakfasts to keep them going longer in the classroom. They're especially good for hiding the oils needed when eating a plant-based diet, which children won't always willingly eat.

Green Smoothie

SERVES 2

1 cup frozen mango cubes
2 cups kale or baby spinach leaves
2 tablespoons green powdered supplement
  of your choice (see notes on our pantry)
3 tablespoons coconut oil
1 tablespoon chia seeds
1 cup ice cubes
1 scoop plant-based protein powder

Place all the ingredients in a blender or food processor and blend until smooth.

Chocolate Almond Smoothie

SERVES 2

⅓ cup almond butter
2 frozen bananas, roughly chopped
3 tablespoons flaxseed oil
2 teaspoons cacao powder
1 cup ice cubes
1 avocado, peeled and seeded
2 servings of plant-based protein powder

Place all the ingredients and 1 cup water in a blender or food processor and blend until smooth.

CHOCOLATE ALMOND SMOOTHIE
See page 31

GREEN SMOOTHIE
See page 31

Light Quickies

Snacks are often are the biggest traps when considering what foods might be causing issues with weight, fatigue or reactions. This is because we often wait until we are really really 'hangry' and then grab the nearest bar/drink/chips/cake and shove it in as quick as it will go, probably while still staring at our screens.

The trick here is to be prepared and to be present when we eat – and it does not take much effort.

BY HAVING:

cut up vegetable sticks with a hummus dip
rice crackers with nut butter spread or avocado
a combination of activated nuts and seeds
or the humble apple (preferably organic)

Having these close by, either in our home or work fridge, we will be much less likely to feed ourselves empty, nutrition-less food. These are really quick and really easy – so much so that there are no recipes in this book for them – but that doesn't mean they are any less important to take note of.

Experiment with turning off the screen and focusing just on the act of eating at these times and you might find you get the full amount of energy your food is designed to give you, because you are engaging in digestion in the true sense of it.

TWO

NOURISH
YOURSELF

NOURISH YOURSELF

Inspired by dishes throughout South-east Asia, the recipes in this chapter combine traditional meals with contemporary tweaks. Often, we associate Asian meals with convenient takeaway that is high in artificial flavours or preservatives and can leave us feeling a little worse for wear. These recipes show you how easy it is to ditch the pre-made sauces and pastes, and create your own naturally. We promise they taste just as good, if not better, and have the bonus of being beneficial to your health.

From Japan to Thailand, there is such a wonderful variety of herbs and spices in Asian cooking. They all carry vibrant flavours and their own health benefits, whether it be aiding digestion, decreasing inflammation or helping stimulate circulation. You will find everything from quick, refreshing salads to hearty curries, many of which complement each other ... and lots and lots of vegetables, but presented in so many different ways we are sure your taste buds will be delighted!

The dishes can be served alone or combine some of the smaller ones and present them as a smorgasbord. This is especially good when you are having people around to share a meal.

You may need to buy some of the ingredients from your local Asian grocer, but sometimes this can be part of the fun – while you are there you will discover a whole range of new foods!

FOR THE LOVE OF A GOOD WRAP

*Wraps cannot be overlooked for the cook who wants fast,
accessible AND tasty food. They are so easy to throw
together and with so many ways to roll food up, and even
more ways to fill the wraps, they are a perfect way
to combine flavours and nutrients.*

Kale Collard Wraps

We can let go of the idea that we need to use traditional grain-based wraps for our food. Embrace the use of collard greens, lettuce leaves, kale leaves, cabbage leaves – any of the wide 'flattish' leaves work well and each one brings a unique flavour and texture. These collard green wraps are perfect for an afternoon snack and the hint of zesty orange really brings them to life.

SERVES 2

1 bunch collard leaves (such as Chinese
  broccoli leaves or silverbeet leaves)
2 tablespoons coconut oil
½ teaspoon curry powder
4 garlic cloves, crushed
1 teaspoon grated orange zest
juice of ½ orange
1 tablespoon maple syrup

4 cups kale leaves, washed and roughly chopped
pinch of salt
1 avocado, sliced
1 carrot, cut into ribbons with a peeler
1 cup fermented vegetables, purchased
  (or see page 143)
large handful coriander leaves, roughly chopped

You can use the leaves fresh or blanch them, if preferred. To do this, pour boiling water into a large bowl. Add 1 collard leaf at a time to the bowl and hold in the water for 10 seconds. Remove the blanched leaves to a plate and set aside to cool.

Heat the coconut oil in a large frying pan. Add the curry powder, garlic, orange zest, orange juice and maple syrup and cook, stirring, for 2–3 minutes. Add the kale and salt and cook for another 2 minutes, stirring well. Remove from the heat and set aside.

Place the collard leaves on a flat surface and top with the kale mixture, avocado, carrot, fermented vegetables and coriander. Roll up into a wrap and serve.

Roasted Coconut Betel Leaves

Often chewed after meals thoughout India and South-east Asia, the betel leaf has antibacterial and anti-inflammatory properties, and contains an essential oil that aids digestion and gives it a wonderful fresh flavour. They may be small, but they form the basis for perfect bite-sized starters, sure to impress your dinner party guests. You can find them in Asian grocers.

SERVES 4

½ cup coconut flakes
100 g tempeh, finely diced
3 tablespoons tamari
juice of ½ lime
1 teaspoon coconut oil
6 spring onions, sliced lengthways
  into thin 3–4 cm strips
20 betel leaves, rinsed and dried
1 cup shredded mint
1 cup kimchi (purchased or see page 141)
3 kaffir lime leaves, thinly sliced

Preheat the oven to 180°C. Line a baking tray with baking paper.

Spread out the coconut on the prepared tray and roast for 5 minutes or until golden brown.

Combine the tempeh, tamari and lime juice in a small bowl. Heat the coconut oil in a large frying pan over medium heat. Add the tempeh mixture and cook, stirring, for 5 minutes or until golden. Remove from the pan and set aside.

Add the spring onion to the pan and cook for 2–3 minutes or until soft.

Lay the betel leaves flat on a serving platter. Top with the tempeh mixture, mint, kimchi, roasted coconut flakes and lime leaf.

These are bite-sized so you only need a tiny amount of each topping, but together they give a great burst of flavour.

Panko Crusted Spinach Avocado Sushi Rolls

This roll is based on a tuna sushi roll from Sensei in Maui. Tracy used to love ordering this roll every time she visited the beautiful island of Maui and this is her version, recreating a similar, delicious experience! You can choose to have the more traditional version by omitting the frying stage, but if you are looking for something a little different, try the deep-fried version just like the one you will find in Hawaii.

SERVES 4

2 cups sushi rice
4 tablespoons sushi vinegar (you can buy this or you can make your own by combining 2 tablespoons rice vinegar and 1 tablespoon sugar and stirring together until the sugar dissolves)
salt
4 nori sheets
about 20 baby spinach leaves
1 avocado, sliced
fermented vegetables or Japanese pickles
coconut oil, for frying
1½ cups panko breadcrumbs
tamari, for dipping
pickled ginger and wasabi, to serve (optional)

Tempura Batter
1⅔ cups plain flour
1½ cups cornflour
2 cups sparkling water, plus extra if needed
1–2 teaspoons salt

Wash and drain the rice. Place the rice and 2½ cups water in a small saucepan. Bring to the boil, then reduce the heat to low and simmer, covered, for 20 minutes or until all the water has been absorbed. (Or follow the instructions on the sushi rice packet).

Allow the rice to cool. Add the sushi vinegar and toss to combine with a rice paddle. Salt lightly.

Lay one sheet of nori, shiny-side down, on a sushi mat or board. Spread about ¾ cup rice over the nori, leaving a 1.5 cm border all round.

Lay about 5 baby spinach leaves and a couple slices of avocado across the bottom, followed by the fermented veggies or Japanese pickles. Using a finger, wet the nori edges closest to you and furthest away from you. Using either your hands or the bamboo sushi roller, roll the nori away from you into a tight roll. Wet the edge with a little more water if the roll isn't sealing properly. Repeat with the remaining nori sheets and filling.

If you'd like a more decadent roll, keep going!

To make the batter, combine all the ingredients in a large bowl. If it is too thick, continue to stir or add a little more sparkling water.

Place the panko breadcrumbs on a tray.

Heat the coconut oil in a large frying pan over medium heat. You want to fill the pan to a depth of 2.5 cm. Test the oil by dropping in a pinch of batter. If it burns quickly the oil is too hot; if it browns and sizzles nicely, then it's ready!

Working with one whole roll at a time, dip it into the tempura batter, allowing the excess batter to drip off, and then toss the roll in the panko crumbs to coat evenly. Take care as this process can be very messy!

Place the coated rolls in the hot oil and cook until golden and crispy all over. Remove and drain on a plate lined with paper towel, then season lightly with salt.

Vietnamese Rice Paper Rolls

These are more traditional rolls, but that doesn't make them any less appealing. They're easy to make, everyone loves them and, like all wraps, it's fun to play with the fillings inside. As well as being delicious, they are another wonderful way to get your dose of vegetables.

SERVES 4

60 g dried rice vermicelli noodles, prepared according to packet instructions
½ cup tamari
3 tablespoons sesame oil
½ red chilli, seeded and diced
150 g tempeh, cut into matchsticks
1 Lebanese cucumber, cut into long matchsticks

1 carrot, cut into matchsticks
1 cup bean sprouts
1 cup coriander leaves
1 cup mint leaves
8 × 20 cm rice paper sheets
juice of 1 lime

Place the noodles, half the tamari, half the sesame oil and half the chilli in a large bowl and toss to combine.

Heat the remaining sesame oil in a frying pan. Add the tempeh and cook for 3–5 minutes or until brown. Set aside.

Have the rest of all the ingredients laid out on separate plates.

Fill a large bowl with hot water and, working with 1 rice paper sheet at a time, place it in the bowl for 1 minute or until it is soft. Lay flat on a hard clean surface and, leaving a 2 cm gap on each side, top with small amounts of each ingredient: some noodles, tempeh, cucumber, carrot, bean sprouts, coriander and mint.

Fold the ends in and roll up firmly to enclose the filling.

Repeat with the remaining rice paper sheets and filling ingredients.

Combine the remaining tamari and chilli with the lime juice in a small bowl. Serve with the rolls as a dipping sauce.

Crispy Asparagus Wraps

These asparagus wraps are simple to make, but are special enough to look like they took some effort. They make a pretty and tasty side dish or starter. Wonton wrappers can be found in the refrigerated section of the supermarket, usually near the fresh pasta. Make sure you choose ones without egg if you are 100% plant-based. Top with purple and green micro greens for an extra special touch.

MAKES 24

24 wonton wrappers
1 tablespoon Dijon mustard
1 tablespoon rice syrup or maple syrup
12 asparagus spears, woody ends removed
extra virgin olive oil, for frying
salt
micro greens, to serve (optional)

Place 1 wonton wrapper on a clean benchtop and spread with a very thin layer of mustard and syrup. Place another wrapper on top.

Place 1 asparagus spear diagonally on top of the wonton wrapper. Wet the corner closest to the asparagus and roll the spear up into a tight spiral. Use a little water on your fingertip to seal the wrapper closed.

Repeat with remaining wrappers, mustard, syrup and asparagus.

Heat enough oil to generously cover the base of a large frying pan over medium heat. When the oil is hot, add the asparagus wraps, a few at a time and cook, turning, until brown and crispy on all sides. Remove and drain on a plate lined with paper towel. Repeat with the remaining wraps.

Season with salt and serve hot, sprinkled with micro greens (if using).

Asian-inspired Tacos

Who doesn't like tacos? Brilliant for a casual get-together. This twist on Mexican lets people have some fun while filling their tortillas with some interesting flavours. For the tortillas, either buy a good-quality brand (with the least amount of ingredients) or make your own as below.

SERVES 4

chilli sauce (see page 109), to serve

Tortillas
⅓ cup chickpea (besan) flour
2 cups water
pinch of salt
2 tablespoons extra virgin olive oil

Slaw
½ Chinese cabbage, thinly sliced
2 spring onions, thinly sliced
4 cm piece of ginger, peeled
  and cut into thin strips
3 jalapeno chillies, thinly sliced
1 bunch coriander, leaves and stems
  roughly chopped
⅔ cup cashew nuts, chopped

Dressing
juice of 1 lime.
3 kaffir lime leaves, sliced
2 garlic cloves, crushed
1 red chilli, finely chopped
½ cup soy sauce

Guacamole Mix
2 avocados, roughly mashed
3 jalapeno chillies, seeded and sliced
juice of 1 lime
1 bunch of coriander, leaves and stems
  roughly chopped

Grilled Baby Corn
½ teaspoon paprika
½ teaspoon ground cumin
½ teaspoon ground coriander
pinch of freshly ground black pepper
grated zest of 1 lime
salt and pepper
3–4 cups baby corn, halved lengthways
coconut oil, for frying

For the tortillas, combine the flour, water, salt and half the oil in a bowl. Rest for 20 minutes.

Heat a small frying pan over medium–high heat and add 1 teaspoon oil . When the pan is hot but the oil is not smoking, add ¼ cups of the batter and cook for 1–2 minutes. Flip and cook the other side for another 1–2 minutes. Wrap in foil and keep warm in a low oven while you cook the remaining tortillas.

To make the slaw, combine all the ingredients in a large bowl.

To make the dressing, whisk together all the ingredients and add to the slaw. Toss to coat.

To make the guacamole, place all the ingredients in a medium bowl and mix to combine.

To prepare the grilled corn, combine the spices, lime zest and seasoning in a medium bowl and set aside.

Heat a frying pan over medium–high heat, add the corn and cook for 3–4 minutes, turning occasionally. Add the corn to the spice mix and toss until the corn is well coated.

Place all the elements on the table and allow everyone to serve themselves, filling their tortillas with slaw, corn, guacamole and chilli sauce.

Eggplant San Choy Bow

San choy bow is an Asian classic. In this version, we experiment with different plant-based fillings and greens (or purples!) as the wrap.

SERVES 2-3

1 cup cauliflower florets, diced
1 eggplant, finely diced
1 tablespoon coconut oil, melted
200 g canned chickpeas, drained and rinsed
1 cup coriander leaves, roughly chopped
3 tablespoons shredded coconut
½ teaspoon salt

1 teaspoon grated lemon zest
1 teaspoon sesame oil
1 teaspoon sesame seeds
1 teaspoon soy sauce
6 large lettuce leaves, such as butter, iceberg or radicchio

Preheat the oven to 180°C. Line a baking tray with baking paper.

Coat the cauliflower and eggplant in coconut oil and place on the prepared tray. Roast for about 20 minutes or until the edges are lightly browned.

Transfer to a large bowl and add the remaining ingredients, except the lettuce leaves. Mix together well.

Spoon the mixture into the lettuce leaf cups and serve.

NOT TO OVERLOOK A GOOD SALAD

We could make a whole book just dedicated to salads.
Thank goodness we have moved past the basic lettuce
and tomato combo – these days salads are an opportunity
to combine more hearty grains, nuts and seeds, and
of course the brilliant dressings that bring them to life.

Snow Pea Salad

This salad is incredibly light and fresh, making it the perfect side to almost any dish. Black sesame seeds bring with them an exceptionally high amount of antioxidants and anti-aging benefits as well as the normal high mineral content found in all sesame seeds: iron, calcium, zinc and magnesium.

SERVES 4

½ Chinese cabbage, thinly sliced
1 bunch watercress, leaves picked
150 g snow peas, cut diagonally in half
100 g snow pea sprouts
1 red capsicum, sliced into matchsticks
½ cup white or black sesame seeds

Dressing
3 tablespoons sesame oil
2 tablespoons mirin
100 ml tamari
1 red chilli, seeded and finely chopped
2 tablespoons grated ginger

Combine the cabbage, watercress, snow peas, sprouts , capsicum and sesame seeds in a large bowl and set aside for 10 minutes to allow the flavours to infuse.

To make the dressing, whisk together all the ingredients in a small bowl.

Drizzle the dressing over the salad and gently toss to coat.

This is best served really cold and fresh.

Kelp Noodle Salad with Carrot Dressing

Kelp noodles are wonderful to have in your cupboard for those nights you don't feel like cooking, and want to just whip a bunch of ingredients together to make a meal. Kelp is a seaweed and often a staple in Asian cultures because of its high amounts of trace minerals including Iodine. Iodine is required for proper functioning of our thyroid gland and due to farming practices today, our soil is often low in iodine – meaning our foods are, and in turn – we are! These noodles help combat that problem naturally and with this sauce, they taste great too!

SERVES 2–4

1 x 450 g packet kelp noodles
1 bunch bok choy, bases trimmed,
  coarsely chopped
4 big cabbage leaves and shredded
3 carrots, thinly sliced on the diagonal
1 bunch mint leaves, picked

Carrot Dressing
⅓ cup coconut milk
½ teaspoon ground turmeric

2 cm piece of ginger, peeled and chopped
3 carrots, chopped
⅓ cup extra virgin olive oil
½ teaspoon salt
2 tablespoons toasted sesame oil
1 tablespoon maple syrup
½ cup brown rice vinegar
½ red onion, roughly chopped
2 tablespoons water

To make the dressing, place all the ingredients in a blender or food processor and blend until well combined but still with a little texture from the carrots.

Place the noodles, bok choy, cabbage, carrot and mint in a large bowl. Add the dressing and toss to combine.

Orchard Street Raw Pad Thai

Orchard Street is a Bondi cafe – and movement. Naturopath Kirstin Shanks' elixirs and meals are exquisite and the epitome of health and wellness. Here is her famous raw Pad Thai. You will need to start this recipe a few hours ahead as the cashews need to soak first.

SERVES 6

1 red chilli, sliced into thin rings
¼ bunch Thai basil, leaves only
¼ bunch coriander, leaves only

Tamari Coriander Cashews
2 cups cashews, soaked in water for 2–4 hours, rinsed and drained
3 tablespoons tamari, warmed
2 tablespoons ground coriander
(Orchard St also uses ½ teaspoon St Marys Thistle Powder, which is great if you can source it!)

Salad
2 x 450 g packets kelp noodles
500 g carrot, julienned

250 g parsnip, julienned
500 g zucchini, spirilised (if you don't have a spiriliser cut them into thick strips)
2 bunches Chinese broccoli, cut into thick strips
100 g sugar peas, halved

Sauce
¾ cup almond butter
juice of 2 limes
2 kaffir lime leaves
4 tablespoons tamari
½ lemongrass stem, inside part only, bruised
¾ cup water
1 teaspoon toasted sesame oil

To make the tamari cashews, combine the nuts, tamari and coriander in a bowl and set aside for 2 hours. Preheat the oven to the lowest possible temperature. Spread out the cashews on a baking tray and dry-roast them, leaving the door open a crack if possible. If you do have a dehydrator, dry them for 36 hours.

For the salad, soak the kelp noodles in water for 30 minutes. Rinse well.

Place all the salad ingredients in a big bowl and mix together well.

To prepare the sauce, place all the ingredients in a food processor and blend for a few minutes.

Drizzle the sauce over the salad and toss it through.

To serve, top the salad with sliced chilli, basil and coriander leaves and the crunchy cashews.

BBQ Tempeh and Pineapple Salad

Pineapple is such a tropical fruit, eaten in many different ways throughout South-east Asia; sometimes even with salt and chilli or, like in this recipe, cooked. Not only does it taste good, it is also full of enzymes that are great for digestion and our skin.

SERVES 2–4

½ cup soy sauce
2 tablespoons grated ginger
1 teaspoon coconut oil, plus extra for frying
1 × 300 g packet tempeh, cut into
 2 cm thick slices
1 ripe pineapple, peeled and sliced
 into thin wedges
1 red onion, thinly sliced
4 kaffir lime leaves, thinly sliced
Pinch of salt
2 cups shredded iceberg lettuce
juice of 2 limes, plus extra lime halves to serve

Combine the soy sauce, ginger and coconut oil in a medium bowl. Add the tempeh and turn to coat. Set aside for 5 minutes.

Heat a little coconut oil in a frying pan or chargrill pan over medium–high heat. Add the tempeh and pineapple in batches and cook for 3–4 minutes on each side.

Place the pineapple in a large bowl with the onion and kaffir lime and season with salt. (The mix of salty and sweet here is divine!) Add the shredded lettuce, tempeh and lime juice and toss tightly to combine. Alternatively, arrange the salad on a bed of lettuce as shown in the photo. Serve with extra lime halves for squeezing over.

Watermelon and Asian Herb Salad

Watermelon is normally best eaten by itself, but every now and then it's nice to mix it up and serve it in a salad. I can think of no better accompaniments than the herbs of Asia and this to-die-for dressing.

SERVES 4

1 large sweet potato, peeled and very thinly sliced
400 g watermelon, cut into medium chunks
1 bunch mint, leaves roughly torn
1 bunch coriander, leaves roughly torn
½ bunch Thai basil, leaves roughly torn
4 spring onions, cut into julienne
1 Lebanese cucumber, cut into chunks
pepper

Dressing
1 bunch coriander, leaves and stalks
1 jalapeno chilli, seeded and roughly chopped
½ cup lime juice
½ cup extra virgin olive oil
1 spring onion, trimmed

Blanch the sweet potato slices in a bowl of boiling water for 4 minutes. Refresh in a bowl of iced water for 4 minutes.

Meanwhile, combine the watermelon, fresh herbs, spring onion, cucumber and a grinding of pepper in a large bowl.

Drain the sweet potato and add it to the salad.

To make the dressing, place all the ingredients in a blender and blend until smooth.

Pour the dressing over the salad and gently toss to combine.

Note
Use a mandolin to slice the sweet potato if you have one

Teriyaki Mixed Grain Salad

This is a hearty salad and an easy way to get vegetables into those who are not so keen to eat them, especially with the homemade teriyaki sauce. Sweet potato packs tremendous nutritional value and helps stabilise blood sugar – and yes, you can find them in different colours! The cauliflower is also wonderful roasted and hosts lots of antioxidants.

SERVES 4

1½ cups cauliflower florets, broken into
  bite-sized pieces
2 cups brussels sprouts, trimmed and quartered
1 large sweet potato (white, purple or orange),
  cut into cubes
extra virgin olive oil, for drizzling
3 tablespoons pine nuts
6 sprigs spring onions, thinly sliced
2 handfuls kale, roughly chopped
2–3 handfuls baby spinach leaves
2–3 fresh mandarins, peeled and segmented,
  or alternatively use 200 g can mandarins, drained
1 handful mung bean or bean sprouts

1½ cups cooked wild rice and farro – or whatever
  grains you have! It's good to mix 2–3 grains
  to add dimension to this salad

Dressing
⅓ cup teriyaki sauce (see page 108)
⅓ cup rice wine vinegar
½ teaspoon garlic powder
½ teaspoon onion powder
½ teaspoon salt
½ teaspoon pepper
2 teaspoons coconut sugar
½ cup olive or sesame oil

Preheat the oven to 200°C. Line a baking tray with baking paper.

Place the cauliflower, brussels sprouts and sweet potato on the prepared tray and toss with a light drizzle of extra virgin olive oil. Roast for 20–25 minutes or until the edges start to colour.

Meanwhile, spread out the pine nuts on a baking tray and lightly roast in the oven for 5 minutes.

To make the dressing, place all the ingredients in a small bowl and whisk together.

Place the roasted vegetables and pine nuts in a large bowl. Add the remaining ingredients and the dressing and toss gently to combine.

Crunchy Spring Noodle Salad

Fried noodles are a street food you find served throughout South-east Asia, especially from little hole-in-the-wall vendors, perfect for a quick bite while wandering through the many exotic markets you can find through the region. While fried food is not something you want to indulge in often, it's fine in small amounts like in this hearty salad and the crisp noodles make for a fanastic contrast.

SERVES 4

2 tablespoons peanut oil
2 cups rice vermicelli noodles
salt
150 g purple cabbage, shredded
150 g green cabbage, shredded
80 g carrots, cut into matchsticks
1 red capsicum, thinly sliced
2 handfuls baby spinach leaves
4 spring onions, thinly sliced

Dressing
½ cup tamari
½ cup lemon juice
1 tablespoon white vinegar
2 tablespoons agave syrup or coconut sugar
2 tablespoons sesame oil
2 tablespoons sunflower oil
salt and pepper

Heat the peanut oil in a large wok or saucepan over high heat.

Break up and separate the rice noodles with your hands. Once the oil is hot (you can test by dropping in a noodle to see if it crisps up straight away) drop a handful of noodles at a time into the hot oil. They will sizzle and crisp up immediately so watch out!

Carefully flip them over to crisp on the other side. Cook for only 30–60 seconds as you only want them to crisp, not to brown. Using a flat strainer or tongs, remove the noodles from the oil and place them on a plate lined with paper towel. Lightly salt them and set aside to cool. Repeat with remaining noodles.

To make the dressing, combine all the ingredients in a bowl.

Place the remaining salad ingredients in a large bowl and add the cooled noodles.

Just before serving, add the dressing to the salad and gently toss to combine.

Creamy Curried Purple Cabbage Salad

Curry powder is an Anglicised kind of masala, or spice mix. Such spice mixes are an intrinsic part of South Asian cuisines and their intense fresh flavours soon became a firm favourite with colonial visitors to the East. The curry powder not only brings a unique flavour to this dish; it is also anti-inflammatory, anti-bacterial and boosts the immune system.

SERVES 2 AS A MAIN OR 4 AS A SIDE

½ cup Veganaise (a vegan mayonnaise that you can buy at most health food stores)
2 tablespoons curry powder
1 small head purple cabbage, thinly sliced
4 spring onions, cut in julienne
⅓ cup currants

½ cup roasted cashew nuts
1 cup fresh or frozen peas (if frozen, let them thaw first; if fresh, blanch them in boiling water for 2–3 minutes)
1 cup cooked quinoa
salt and pepper

Mix together the Veganaise and curry powder and set aside.

Place the remaining ingredients in a large bowl. Add the Veganaise sauce and gently toss to coat. Serve chilled.

Forbidden Rice with Mango, Cashews and Fresh Herbs

Black rice has a rich cultural history; called 'Forbidden' or 'Emperor's' rice, it was reserved for the Emperor in ancient China and used as a tribute food. It is high in antioxidants and has a nuttier flavour and fuller texture than your standard white rice, making it a wonderful ingredient for salads.

SERVES 4

1 cup black rice
1 orange
1½ tablespoons lime juice
1 tablespoon tamari
1 tablespoon extra virgin olive oil
1 firm mango, diced
½ cup mint leaves, roughly chopped
½ cup basil leaves, roughly chopped

3 spring onions, thinly sliced
½ cup roasted cashew nuts, roughly chopped
1 jalapeno chilli, seeded and diced
salt and pepper
2 tablespoons shredded coconut, toasted

Cook the black rice according to the packet instructions. Allow to cool on a large baking tray so the grains stay separate and don't go mushy.

Segment the orange into a bowl, discarding the pith, rind and seeds. Reserve any juice in the bowl.

Add the lime juice, tamari and oil to the orange segments and juice and mix well.

Place the rice, mango, fresh herbs, spring onion, cashews and chilli in a large bowl. Add the orange segments and dressing and gently mix together.

Season with salt and pepper and top with shredded coconut.

Soba Noodle Salad with Greens and Seeds

Soba noodles are a typical Japanese food, and are commonly made with buckwheat, or a combination of buckwheat and wheat. Contrary to what you might think, buckwheat is not related to wheat as it isn't a grass; it is high in essential amino acids and rich in iron and selenium. If you are eating gluten-free, make sure you choose the buckwheat-only variety. This salad can be served warm or cold and the components can all be made a day ahead and tossed together just before serving.

SERVES 4

1 x 250 g packet soba noodles
2 bunches broccolini, trimmed
100 g fresh peas (or thawed frozen peas)
1 teaspoon extra virgin olive oil
300 g button mushrooms, sliced
1 tablespoon tamari
½ bunch basil, leaves finely shredded
½ bunch mint, leaves finely shredded

Dressing
⅓ cup flaxseed oil
⅓ cup tamari
⅓ cup rice wine vinegar
2 teaspoons sesame oil
1 teaspoon grated ginger

Garnish
2 teaspoons white sesame seeds, toasted
2 teaspoons black sesame seeds
tatsoi or shiso micro herb leaves (optional)

Cook the soba noodles according to the packet instructions. Drain and rinse in cold water.

Blanch the broccolini in a large saucepan of boiling water for 1 minute. Add the peas and blanch for 1 minute, then drain and refresh in a bowl of iced water, then drain again.

Heat the oil in a medium frying pan over medium heat, add the mushrooms and tamari and cook for 3–4 minutes or until soft and nicely browned.

To make the dressing, whisk together all the ingredients in a small bowl.

Combine the noodles, broccolini, peas, mushroom, basil and mint in a large bowl, then add the dressing and gently toss to coat. Garnish with the sesame seeds and micro herb leaves (if using).

Alternatively, arrange all the components separately and spoon the dressing over.

WARM DISHES THAT PACK A PUNCH

Despite some of the longer ingredients lists, none of these dishes take too much time to make. We feel they are proof that classic meals can be enjoyed just as much without the animal products.

Thai Hot and Sour Soup with Okra

Lemongrass, mint, coriander and kaffir lime leaves are the key aromatic ingredients used in Asian cooking and their fresh flavours lift every dish. This soup is really an ode to them, with the softer flavour of okra soaking up their intensity.

SERVES 4

8 red shallots, stems peeled
2 lemongrass, white part only, thinly sliced
50 g piece of galangal, peeled and sliced
6 kaffir lime leaves
4 cm piece of turmeric, peeled and thinly sliced
  (or 1 teaspoon ground turmeric)
4 cm piece of ginger, peeled and chopped
4 red chillies, seeded and chopped
1 bunch coriander, roots, stems and leaves
1 litre vegetable stock or water
8 cherry tomatoes, quartered and squashed
2 cups sliced okra (about 20)

To serve
⅓ cup lime juice
⅓ cup coriander leaves
½ cup Vietnamese mint (or regular mint)

Place the shallots, lemongrass, galangal, kaffir lime leaves, turmeric, ginger, chillies and coriander in a food processor and blend to a paste, adding a little water if necessary. Spoon into a large saucepan and cook over medium heat for 5 minutes or until fragrant and dry.

Pour in the stock or water and bring to the boil. Add the tomatoes and cook for 5 minutes, then add the okra and cook for 1 minute. You don't want to overcook the okra as it naturally releases a gel-like substance.

Remove the pan from the heat and add the lime juice and most of the coriander and mint. Ladle the soup into bowls and garnish with the remaining coriander and mint.

Mint and Pea Soup

This soup is so pleasing to everyone we had to include it. It makes a lovely starter for some of the dishes in this book, complementing the mint flavours featured in several other recipes. It also makes the perfect quick lunch, especially if you are doing a cleanse.

SERVES 4

2 tablespoons olive oil
1 small onion, chopped
1 garlic clove, crushed
1 litre vegetable stock
4 cups baby spinach leaves
  or chopped English spinach

1 kg frozen peas, thawed
1 cup mint leaves, roughly chopped
  plus extra to serve
salt and pepper

Heat the oil in a large saucepan over medium heat, add the onion and garlic and cook for 2–3 minutes. Add the stock and bring to the boil, then stir in the spinach, peas and mint and cook for another 3–4 minutes.

Remove the pan from the heat and process in blender until smooth. Season to taste with salt and pepper.

Ladle into bowls, garnish with extra mint leaves and serve.

Pho

This traditional Vietnamese dish is all about the broth. When not using animal products, the trick is to leave herbs and spices in the broth for a longer period so their fragrances and flavours infuse the liquid. The creamy texture of eggplant adds the 'meaty' component to this dish, along with nutrients that are beneficial for our brain. Win-win.

SERVES 4

1 teaspoon coconut oil
3 tablespoons miso paste
3 tablespoons tamari
8 baby eggplants, halved lengthways
  and thickly sliced
1 x 250 g packet flat dried rice noodles
4 spring onions, thinly sliced
1 bunch Thai basil, leaves roughly chopped
1 bunch coriander, leaves roughly chopped
1 bunch mint, leaves roughly chopped
3 red chillies, thinly sliced
2 cups bean sprouts
2 limes, cut into wedges
chilli sauce (see page 109), to serve

Broth
150 g piece of ginger, peeled
  and roughly chopped
2 brown onions, peeled and halved
10 star anise
6 cinnamon quills
6 cardamom pods
5 cloves
2 tablespoons coriander seeds
3 litres vegetable stock
2 tablespoons rice syrup
½ cup tamari

To make the broth, heat the coconut oil in a large frying pan over medium heat, add the ginger and onion and cook for 5 minutes, or until nicely browned. Set aside.

In a separate frying pan, dry-roast all the dried spices over low heat for 3–5 minutes or until fragrant. Cool, then place them in a 'nut milk' bag or a piece of muslin tied with string.

Pour the stock into a large saucepan, add the ginger and onion, rice syrup, tamari and the bag of spices. Bring to the boil, then reduce the heat to low and simmer gently for an hour. (If you have the time, leave it to infuse for an extra 1–2 hours off the heat.)

Preheat the oven to 180°C. Line a baking tray with baking paper.

Mix together the tamari and miso in a medium bowl, add the eggplant and turn to coat well. Marinate for 5 minutes, then arrange the eggplant on the prepared tray. Bake for about 20 minutes or until browned.

Cook the noodles according to the packet instructions. Drain and divide evenly among 4 large bowls. Top with the eggplant.

Place the spring onion, fresh herbs and chilli in separate bowls for people to add to their dish as desired.

Ladle over the hot broth (leaving out the large pieces of onion and ginger) and top with bean sprouts and a squeeze of lime.

Serve with chilli sauce.

A Father's Congee

As a single-parent, Gemma's father went from hardly knowing how to cook a meal to lovingly serving his family beautiful, nourishing dishes. This is one of those dishes. It's light and a little on the salty-side, making it the perfect alternative to the original vegetable soup we often crave when we're unwell. Snake beans are popular in South-east Asia. We include them here to add protein as well as folate and other antioxidants.

SERVES 4

1 cup basmati rice
2½ litres vegetable stock
4 garlic cloves, crushed or chopped
2 cm piece of ginger, peeled and finely chopped
2 bunches snake beans, thinly sliced
1 bunch bok choy, chopped
2 carrots, thinly sliced
½ teaspoon pepper

To Serve
1 bunch coriander, leaves picked
1 red chilli, seeded and sliced
1 cup bean sprouts

Combine the rice and stock in a large saucepan over low heat and simmer for 45 minutes, stirring often. Add more water if the mixture becomes gluggy – it should have a soupy consistency.

Add the garlic, ginger, beans, boy choy, carrot and pepper and simmer for another 5 minutes.

Serve topped with the fresh coriander, chilli and bean sprouts.

Jessica Gomes' Bibimbap Bowl

Long-time friends Jessica Gomes and Gemma spent time together working in Korea where they fell in love with the bibimbap bowls. So that they could recreate them at home they came up with these two versions (see also page 94). Make sure you have the sauces – they absolutely make the bowls!

SERVES 2

1 teaspoon coconut oil
1 cup dried porcini mushrooms, soaked
  and rimmed before cooking
4 cups baby spinach leaves or chopped
  English spinach
2 nori sheets, halved and thinly sliced
⅓ cup kimchi (purchased or see page 141)
1 cup cooked black rice

To serve
cashew sauce (see page 109)
chilli sauce (see page 109)

Heat the coconut oil in a medium wok, add the mushrooms and cook, stirring, for 5 minutes or until browned. Remove from the wok. Add the spinach and cook for 1 minute or until wilted.

Divide the mushroom and spinach between 2 bowls, add the nori, kimchi and rice and serve with the cashew and chilli sauces.

Nourishing Bibimbap Bowl

This bowl uses a pickled carrot and daikon mix, which is great to have in the fridge to add as a side to many meals. Arame is a type of seaweed that is dense in micronutrients and comes dried in a packet – it's super good in this bowl. Don't forget the sauces to serve!

SERVES 2

1 cup dried arame
1 tablespoon coconut oil
1 bunch purple kale, stalks removed
  and roughly chopped
1 cup pickled carrot and daikon
  (see page 97)

1 cup bean sprouts
1 cup cooked red or wild rice

To serve
cashew sauce (see page 109)
chilli sauce (see page 109)

Place the arame in a bowl of boiling water, then cover and blanch for 2 minutes. Drain well.

Massage the coconut oil into the kale leaves, scrunching it around with your hands so it goes slightly soft. Place in a medium frying pan over medium heat and cook for about 3 minutes.

Divide the kale mixture and arame between 2 bowls. Add the pickled carrot and daikon mix, bean sprouts and rice and serve with the cashew and chilli sauces.

Pickled Carrot and Daikon

These pickled beauties are found in many Vietnamese dishes, with varying levels of salty, sour or sweet intensity. We think this is the perfect balance. If you have one, use a mandolin to make it easier to get the strips uniformly fine.

MAKES 1–2 JARS

1 litre warm water
⅓ cup white vinegar
3 tablespoons sugar

1 tablespoon salt
3 large carrots, sliced into matchsticks
2 daikon radishes, sliced into matchsticks

In a large bowl, mix the water, vinegar, sugar and salt until the sugar and salt have dissolved.

Combine the carrots and daikon in a large bowl, then spoon into 1–2 clean glass jars tightly packing them as you go. Pour in the vinegar mixture, making sure the vegetables are completely covered, then screw the lids on securely.

Leave in the fridge for 3–5 days before eating. The pickle will keep in the fridge for four weeks.

Tofu Protein Balls

Just like the handy bliss ball that nourishes the body with a heap of nutrients, these tofu balls are full of protein and micronutrients, from the delicious combination of tofu, chickpeas and wakame flakes. So moreish, without tasting 'healthy'!

SERVES 4

Balls

1 x 400 g can chickpeas, drained and rinsed (or even better, cook fresh ones if you have the time!)
200 g organic firm tofu, grated
2 garlic cloves, crushed
2 cm piece of ginger, peeled and finely grated
3 spring onions, thinly sliced
1 bunch coriander, finely chopped
1 tablespoon white miso paste
2 tablespoons wakame or nori flakes
dash of sesame oil

Sauce

100 ml flaxseed oil
140 ml tamari
2 tablespoons mirin

To serve

2 tablespoons black sesame seeds
1 tablespoons nori flakes

To make the balls, blend the chickpeas in a food processor or blender, then transfer to a large bowl. Add the tofu, garlic, ginger, spring onion, coriander, miso and wakame or nori flakes and mix well, using a fork to mash to a smoother consistency if necessary.

Roll into 10–12 small balls with your hands.

Heat the sesame oil in a large frying pan for a couple of minutes until really hot. Add the balls and cook for 2–3 minutes each side or until nicely browned all over.

Meanwhile, to make the sauce, combine all the ingredients in a bowl.

Sprinkle the sesame seeds and nori flakes onto a plate. Place the hot balls on top and serve with the bowl of dipping sauce.

Water Chestnut Yellow Curry with Coconut Topping and Turmeric Quinoa

One of the wonderful aspects of Asian-inspired cooking is the spices. Cumin, coriander, turmeric and cardamom are not only tasty, they also are anti-inflammatory, good for your immune system and aid digestion. When making a curry it's easy to fall into the trap of thinking it's hard to make the paste from scratch and buying pre-made pastes instead – but once you try this, you will realise it isn't hard at all, and some real magic happens when you combine the spices and herbs yourself.

SERVES 4

Curry Paste
2 tablespoons coriander seeds
1 tablespoon cumin seeds
10 cardamom pods
4 red chillies, chopped
5 garlic cloves, crushed
6 red shallots, chopped
8 cm piece of turmeric, peeled and chopped
6 cm piece of galangal, peeled and chopped
grated zest and juice of 1 lime
2 tablespoons tamari
1 bunch coriander
½ cup water

Turmeric Quinoa
1½ cups quinoa
3 cups vegetable stock
2 teaspoons ground turmeric

Coconut and Cashew Topping
½ cup finely shredded or desiccated coconut
½ cup sesame seeds
½ cup tamari almonds, chopped
½ cup roasted cashew nuts, chopped
½ bunch Thai basil, stems removed

Curry
2 x 400 ml cans coconut cream
2 tablespoons rice syrup
½ cup tamari
20 kaffir lime leaves
1 cauliflower, roughly chopped
1 small butternut pumpkin, peeled, seeded and diced
1 x 225 g can water chestnuts, drained and rinsed

To prepare the curry paste, dry-roast the coriander seeds, cumin seeds and cardamom pods in a frying pan for 3–5 minutes or until fragrant.

Transfer to a blender or food processor, add the remaining curry paste ingredients and blend until smooth.

To make the turmeric quinoa, rinse the quinoa thoroughly. Place in a large saucepan, cover with the stock and mix in the turmeric. Bring to the boil, then reduce heat and simmer for 20 minutes or until all the stock has been absorbed and the quinoa is nice and fluffy.

To make the topping, heat a medium frying pan over medium heat, add the coconut, sesame seeds and nuts and dry-fry for 3 minutes, stirring, until fragrant. Set aside.

To prepare the curry, pour the coconut cream into a large saucepan and heat over medium heat for 2–3 minutes. Add the curry paste and simmer, stirring, for 5 minutes.

Add the remaining curry ingredients to the pan and simmer for 20 minutes or until tender.

Serve the curry on top of the quinoa, sprinkled with the nut topping and basil leaves.

Green Curry with Cauliflower Rice

Cauliflower rice is super easy and can be a great way to include this immune-boosting vegetable in your diet. Bamboo shoots are popular in many South-east Asian cuisines as they soak up the flavours of the dish beautifully.

SERVES 4

2 cm piece of ginger, peeled and chopped
2 garlic cloves, crushed
1 red chilli, seeded and finely chopped
4 kaffir lime leaves
1 stem lemongrass, white part only, chopped
1 teaspoon ground coriander
1 teaspoon ground cardamom
1 teaspoon ground turmeric
2 spring onions, sliced
1 teaspoon coconut oil
dash of tamari, plus extra to serve
1 × 400 ml can coconut cream

½ small pumpkin, peeled, seeded and diced
1 cup chopped green beans
½ head broccoli, roughly chopped
2 curry leaves
1 × 225g can bamboo shoots, drained
1 cauliflower, roughly chopped
juice of 1 lime
1 cup cashew nuts, roasted and chopped
1 bunch coriander, leaves and stems
  roughly chopped
lime wedges, to serve (optional)

Place the ginger, garlic, chilli, lime leaves, lemongrass, ground spices, spring onion, coconut oil and tamari in a food processor and blend for a few minutes until smooth.

Transfer the mixture to a large saucepan, add the coconut cream, pumpkin, beans, broccoli, curry leaves and bamboo shoots. Bring to the boil, then reduce the heat to low and simmer for 10 minutes or until the pumpkin is tender.

Meanwhile, place the cauliflower in a food processor and pluse until to a rice-like consistency.

Heat a wok or large frying pan over medium heat, add the cauliflower rice and cook for 4–5 minutes or until lightly browned.

Just before serving, stir the lime juice and a little extra tamari into the curry.

Serve the curry on top of the cauliflower rice, garnished with chopped cashews and coriander, with lime wedges on the side, if liked.

Balinese Satay Roast Sweet Potato

Roast sweet potato is such a brilliant main ingredient, and so simple. Just roast them whole in the oven and enjoy with other vegetables and any flavourings you like. Here we've included Balinese flavours in a delicious satay sauce.

SERVES 4

Roast Sweet Potatoes and Vegetables
4 sweet potatoes
2 cups broccoli florets or broccolini
1 cup podded edamame beans
4 spring onions, thinly sliced
½ cup chopped macadamias (roasted, if liked)

Sauce
½ cup macadamia butter (or you can use almond or cashew butter)
2 garlic cloves, chopped
2 teaspoons coconut sugar
½ cup coconut milk, plus extra if needed
2 teaspoons grated ginger
1 tablespoon tamari
2 teaspoons rice wine vinegar
½ teaspoon chilli flakes
juice of 1 lime

Preheat the oven to 200°C. Line a baking tray with baking paper.

Poke the sweet potatoes with a fork, then wrap them in foil and place on the prepared tray. Bake for 45–60 minutes or until soft when pierced with a fork.

Meanwhile, to make the sauce, place all the ingredients in a food processor or blender and blend until smooth. Add more coconut milk or water to thin the sauce if it seems a little thick. Set aside.

Just before you are ready to serve, steam the broccoli for 2 minutes. Add the edamame to the broccoli and steam for another 2 minutes.

Unwrap the sweet potatoes and slice them lengthways down the centre. Open them out and fill with the steamed veggies. Drizzle over the satay sauce and garnish with the spring onion and macadamias.

Nourish Yourself

Veggie Tempura

When travelling through Japan, it's amazing to try all the different vegetable variations, such as lotus which is like a cross between a potato and a coconut. This Asian vegetable is chock full of B vitamins which are essential for good mental health. The lotus flower is synonymous with peace and tranquillity and consuming the root has been said to alleviate stress, headaches and minimise stress levels. Fried foods like this are an occasional delicious indulgence.

SERVES 4

coconut oil, for frying
3–4 cups mixed vegetables, such as sliced
    sweet potato, carrot, green beans, asparagus,
    eggplant, capsicum, mushrooms, broccoli,
    cauliflower and lotus root
1–2 teaspoons salt
dipping sauces, to serve (see page 108),
    or just use plain tamari or sweet chilli sauce

Tempura Batter
1⅔ cups plain flour
1½ cups cornflour
2 cups sparkling water

To make the batter, combine the flours in a large bowl. Add the water and mix through until just combined – the batter will still have a few lumps and this is fine.

Heat the oil in a medium saucepan. Drop a small amount of batter into the hot oil to check if it is ready. If it browns and bubbles straight away then it is ready. Be careful as the oil will spit once the veggies are added.

Individually dip the veggies into the batter, letting any excess batter drip off, then gently lower them into the hot oil. Work in batches of 3–4 pieces at a time so you don't overcrowd the pan.

Turn the veggies in the oil for a few minutes until they are lightly golden all over. Remove with a slotted spoon and drain on a plate lined with paper towels.

Lightly salt the tempura vegetables and serve right away with your choice of dipping sauce.

DIPPING SAUCES

Tentsuyu

This is the traditional dipping sauce for tempura

SINGLE SERVE

2 tablespoons mirin
2 tablespoons tamari
⅔ cup dashi stock (if you don't have dashi
   on hand, you can buy powdered dashi
   or use vegetable stock)

Combine all the ingredients in a small bowl.
This recipe can easily be doubled.

Ponzu sauce

SINGLE SERVE

1 teaspoon agave, sugar or maple syrup.
1 tablespoon yuzu juice
1 tablespoon tamari
1 tablespoon mirin
1 tablespoon rice vinegar
thinly sliced spring onion, to garnish

Combine all the ingredients, except the spring
onion, in a bowl, stirring until the sugar or
syrup has dissolved. Top with the the sliced
spring onion.

Teriyaki Sauce

Homemade is always the best option!

SERVES 2

½ cup soy sauce
⅓ cup sake
½ cup mirin
2 tablespoons sugar

Combine all the ingredients in a bowl.

Cashew Satay Sauce

MAKES 1 JAR

250 g raw cashew nuts
40 g coconut oil, plus extra for frying
3 garlic cloves, diced
1 red chilli, finely chopped
1 cm piece of ginger, peeled and grated
50 g coconut sugar
1 x 400 ml can coconut milk

Place the cashews and coconut oil in a food processor and blend until a paste forms. Set aside.

Heat a dash of coconut oil in a small saucepan, add the garlic, chilli and ginger and cook for 2–3 minutes or until fragrant. Add the cashew paste, coconut sugar and coconut milk and whisk to combine. Simmer gently over low heat for about 10 minutes. Allow to cool for a few minutes.

Remove from the heat and carefully pour the sauce into a food processor and blend until smooth. Add a little water if the sauce seems too thick.

Pour into a small bowl or glass jar.

Chilli Sauce

MAKES 1 JAR

2 ripe tomatoes
5 long red chillies, seeded and finely chopped
2 garlic cloves, crushed
½ cup apple cider vinegar
100 ml rice syrup
2 cm piece of ginger, peeled and grated
1 teaspoon tamari

Place the tomatoes in a large bowl and cover with boiling water for 1 minute. Carefully remove them from the water and peel off the softened skin. Roughly chop the flesh.

Transfer the tomato to a medium saucepan, add the remaining ingredients and a dash of water and simmer, stirring often, for 15 minutes or until well combined and syrupy.

Pour into a small bowl or glass jar.

CHILLI SAUCE
See page 109

Kimchi Fried Rice

Fried rice is one of those dishes you can whip up after a busy day when you don't know what else to make. Everyone loves it. It is eaten throughout Asia, and this is our play on it, bringing in the much-loved kimchi flavours. It's a great way to use up leftover cooked rice, and feel free to add any extra vegetables you may have in your fridge.

SERVES 4

2 cups jasmine rice (or you can use quinoa)
1 tablespoon coconut oil
5 cm piece of ginger, peeled and grated
1 teaspoon sesame oil

1 cup kimchi (purchased or see page 141)
1 cup fresh peas (or thawed frozen peas)
½ cup tamari
2 spring onions, sliced on the diagonal

Cook the rice or quinoa according to the packet instructions and set aside to cool completely.

Heat the coconut oil in a wok or large frying pan over medium heat and gently cook the ginger for 1 minute or until fragrant.

Add the rice or quinoa, sesame oil, kimchi, peas and tamari and cook for 3 minutes or until heated through. Top with spring onion to serve.

Mushroom Chinese Stir-fry

This Chinese stir-fry uses a range of mushrooms, making it a dish packed with protein and Vitamin D which we need for our moods, and also helps the body absorb calcium, making it an essential nutrient for bone health.

SERVES 4

1 × 270 g packet dried soba noodles (if you are gluten-free look for buckwheat options)
2 tablespoons sesame oil
2 garlic cloves, thinly sliced
1 green chilli, seeded and finely chopped
1 bunch snake beans, thinly sliced
2 bunches Chinese broccoli, chopped
100 g oyster mushrooms

200 g enoki mushrooms
200 g shimeji mushrooms
200g shiitake mushrooms, halved or quartered
½ cup tamari
½ teaspoon Chinese five spice
⅓ cup roasted cashew nuts
fried shallots, to serve

Cook the noodles according to the packet instructions. Drain.

Meanwhile, heat the oil in a large wok, add the garlic, chilli and snake beans and stir-fry for 2 minutes.

Add the Chinese broccoli and mushrooms and cook, tossing frequently for 5–7 minutes or until the mushrooms are tender and lightly browned. Add the tamari and Chinese five spice.

Add the drained noodles to the wok and toss over the heat for another minute until combined. Sprinkle with the roasted cashews and fried shallots and serve.

Shiitake Gnocchi with Shichimi

This super-simple dish relies on two things: using good-quality ingredients and eating it as soon as it's ready. Combining traditional Italian gnocchi and classic Asian flavours may seem a little unusual, but we can't get enough of it. It's the perfect meal to share with a glass of wine.

SERVES 2

3 tablespoons peanut oil
1 bunch Chinese broccoli, roughly chopped
200 g fresh shiitake mushrooms, sliced
1 teaspoon brown rice vinegar
1 teaspoon rice syrup
2 teaspoons shichimi togarashi
  (Japanese seasoning)
1 × 500 g packet gnocchi

Bring a large saucepan of water to the boil.

Meanwhile, heat 1 tablespoon of the peanut oil in a large frying pan over medium–high heat. Add the Chinese broccoli and mushrooms and cook for 3–4 minutes or until soft and the mushrooms are slightly brown.

Place the vinegar, rice syrup, shichimi togarashi and remaining oil in a small bowl and mix together well.

Cook the gnocchi in the boiling water according to the packet instructions Drain, then add to the vegetables. Drizzle the oil mix over the top and mix through gently. Serve immediately.

Miso Roasted Mushrooms

The Japanese have been utilising miso for thousands of years, bringing fermented foods into so many dishes because miso is so versatile. High in nutrients and fantastic for your gut, it's the perfect way to add flavour to any of your vegetables. In this case, it's mushrooms!

SERVES 2

⅓ cup mirin
⅓ cup tamari
2 tablespoons brown miso paste
4 cups portobello, button and crimini mushrooms, sliced, halved or quartered

1 small brown onion, sliced
extra virgin olive oil, for drizzling
1 cup hot cooked brown rice
lemon wedges and micro greens, to serve

Preheat the oven to 200°C. Line a baking tray with baking paper.

Place the mirin, tamari and miso in a small bowl and mix until combined.

Lay a large sheet of foil on the bench (it should be large enough to enclose all the mushrooms in a pouch). Arrange the mushrooms and onion in the centre and pour over the miso mixture and a drizzle of olive oil. Bring up the edges of the foil and seal to form a pouch. Shake gently to coat ensure all the mushrooms are well coated.

Place the parcel on the prepared tray and bake for 30 minutes or until soft and delicious.

Serve with the brown rice, lemon wedges and a topping of micro greens.

Roasted Cauliflower with White Miso Sauce

If you haven't had cauliflower roasted with coconut oil, you need to stop what you're doing right now, and go heat up the oven. It is amazing! Add miso sauce to the mix and it is melt-in-your-mouth delicious, while also being really high in antioxidants.

SERVES 4

1 cauliflower, cut into small florets
2 tablespoons coconut oil, melted
1 teaspoon of shichimi togarashi
  (Japanese seasoning)
micro shiso leaves, to garnish

Sauce
2 tablespoons tahini
2 tablespoons white miso paste
1 tablespoon brown rice vinegar
1 tablespoon mirin
boiling water, to mix

Preheat the oven to 200°C. Line a baking tray with baking paper.

Place the cauliflower on the prepared tray. Drizzle with the oil and use your hands to coat the cauliflower evenly with the oil. Roast for 20 minutes or until nicely browned on the edges.

To make the sauce, combine all the ingredients in a medium bowl and mix until smooth. Add a dash of boiling water to make a thick sauce consistency.

To serve, spread most of the sauce over a plate and arrange the cauliflower on top. Drizzle the rest of sauce over the top and sprinkle with shichimi and shiso leaves.

Spicy Tofu and Veggies

Tofu is a controversial ingredient due to the high phytoestrogen content – meaning that if you consume *excessive* amounts it can act as oestrogen and too much of this can disrupt your system. But soy itself is not to be feared in a balanced diet; it's still very high in protein, iron and calcium. It is important that you purchase organic tofu though, as many of the crops are becoming genetically modified, which you want to avoid.

SERVES 4

coconut oil, for frying
2 cups mixed mushrooms
2 garlic cloves, finely chopped
3–4 spring onions, thinly sliced
1 bunch bok choy, bases trimmed
2 tablespoons tamari
200 g packet brown rice noodles

Sauce
¾ cup teriyaki sauce (see page 108)
1 tablespoon grated ginger
2 tablespoons mirin
½ cup coconut sugar

Tofu
1 cup fine polenta
1 tablespoon shichimi togarashi
   (Japanese seasoning)
375g firm organic tofu, drained
   and sliced into triangles
brine from 1 x 400 g can chickpeas
   (set aside the chickpeas for another use)

To make the sauce, place all the ingredients in a medium saucepan over medium heat. Bring to the boil, then reduce the heat and simmer for 10 minutes or until thick and syrupy. Remove from heat and set aside.

For the tofu, combine the polenta and shichimi togarashi. In a shallow bowl, coat the tofu in the polenta mixture, then dip into the chickpea brine, then put it back in the polenta mixture a second time.

Heat the enough coconut oil in a large frying pan to cover the base well. Add the tofu triangles and cook until golden and crisp on both sides. Remove the tofu, drain on paper towel. Keep warm.

Heat a little oil in a wok over high heat, add the mushrooms and cook, stirring, until browned. Add the garlic, spring onion, bok choy and tamari and cook, tossing, for a couple of minutes until the bok choy is wilted.

Meanwhile, cook the rice noodles according to the packet instructions. Serve with the veggies, tofu and sauce.

Spicy Kimchi and Brown Rice Noodle Joy

This is a super-quick and easy dish to throw together when you are stretched for time.
Using the kimchi is a quick way to to add flavour, while also nourishing your digestive system.

SERVES 2

1 × 200 g packet brown rice noodles
500 g kimchi (purchased or see page 141)
1 litre vegetable stock
1 cup variety of fresh sliced mushrooms

1 bunch bok choy, chopped
1 handful flat-leaf parsley leaves, chopped
1 handful coriander leaves, chopped
2 handfuls fried shallots

Prepare the brown rice noodles according
to the packet instructions.

Place half the kimchi and half the stock in
a large saucepan over medim heat. Bring to the
boil, then reduce the heat and simmer for a few
minutes. Allow to cool for a few minutes, then
blend in a food processor or blender.

Return the blended mixture to the pan. Add
the remaining kimchi and stock, as well as the
mushrooms. Bring to the boil, then reduce the
heat and simmer for a 2–3 minutes or until the
mushrooms start to soften.

Just before serving, add the noodles, bok choy,
herbs and fried shallots. Add a little water
if you prefer a more soupy consistency.

Tempting Tempeh Loaf

We had to include this loaf as it got so much wonderful feedback on Gemma's blog when she shared her father's partner's recipe. The perfect warming winter dish, its full-bodied flavour can be enjoyed by everyone, even those who are gluten-free.

MAKES 1 LOAF

1 cup hulled millet
2 sweet potatoes, peeled and diced
3 tablespoons extra virgin olive oil
1 x 300 g packet tempeh,
   cut into very small cubes
4 garlic cloves, crushed

1 brown onion, finely diced
½ teaspoon each of dried basil,
   sage, thyme and oregano
⅓ cup tamari
3 tablespoons tomato paste

Preheat the oven to 180°C. Line a medium loaf tin with baking paper leaving the sides overhanging.

Place the millet in a saucepan and cover with 2 cups water. Bring to the boil, then reduce the heat and simmer, covered, for 20 minutes or until all the water has been absorbed and the millet is cooked.

Meanwhile steam the sweet potato over a saucepan of simmering water for 10 minutes or until tender. Do not overcook it as it holds the dish together.

Heat the oil in a medium frying pan, add the tempeh and cook for 5 minutes or until lightly browned. Add the garlic, onion and dried herbs and cook for another 5 minutes. Stir in the tamari and tomato paste.

Tip the mixture into a large bowl, add the millet and sweet potato and mash together well. Spoon into in the prepared tin and press firmly.

Bake for 30 minutes or until the loaf is dry to touch. Cut into thick slices and serve warm.

Nasi Goreng with Stir-fried Veggies

A classic Indonesian dish that brings the essence of holidays in Bali to your table at home. It's such a versatile recipe. You can add any extra veggies have on hand – sautéed mushrooms, red capsicum and zucchini work particularly well.

SERVES 4

1 cup red rice
1 teaspoon coconut oil
1 brown onion, diced
1 garlic clove, chopped
2 bunches broccolini, cut into 4cm pieces
2–3 handfuls baby spinach leaves,
   roughly chopped
1 carrot, grated
½ cup torn basil leaves
1 handful fried shallots

4 spring onions, sliced
1 handful roasted cashew nuts

Sauce
½ cup tamari
2 tablespoons rice syrup or alternative
   sweetener of your choice
½ cup chilli sauce (see page 109) or you can use
   store-bought sweet chilli sauce and leave out the
   extra sweetener

Cook the rice according to the packet instructions, then set aside to cool.

To make the sauce, combine all the ingredients in a bowl.

Heat the coconut oil in a large frying pan over medium heat, add the onion and cook for 3 minutes or until soft. Add the garlic and cook for 1–2 minutes or until fragrant.

Add the broccolini and toss for around 3 minutes until heated through. Add the rice and cook, tossing, until heated through.

Add the spinach and toss until it begins to wilt. Add a splash of water any time the rice mixture seems dry. Add half the sauce and toss until heated through.

Before serving, stir through the remaining sauce and the carrot and basil. Spoon into bowls and top with fried shallots, spring onion and roasted cashews.

A LITTLE TO ADD

*A selection of dips and pickled veggies can never go astray
and are always welcome on the side of our plate for flavour
and nutrients!*

Edamame Dip

The soy bean in her true form is a treat to us all. Whether served salty in her pod, with a chilli sauce, or mashed as in this dip, edamame never fails to hit the spot. This vibrant green dip is the perfect starter with fresh vegetable sticks, but it's also wonderful to have in the fridge when you need a snack, especially given its high protein content.

MAKES 2 CUPS

340 g frozen edamame pods
3 tablespoons diced onion
½ cup coriander leaves, roughly chopped
1 garlic clove, sliced
3 tablespoons lemon juice

1 tablespoon miso paste
2 tablespoons sambal oelek (hot chilli paste)
1 teaspoon salt
¼ teaspoon ground black pepper
100 ml extra virgin olive oil

Bring a large saucepan of salted water to the boil, add the edamame and boil for 5 minutes. Drain and rinse under cold water, then remove the edamame from their pods.

Place the edamame, onion, coriander, garlic, lemon juice, miso, sambal oelek, salt and pepper in a food processor. Blend, gradually adding the oil, until the mixture is well combined and reaches a dip consistency. Serve with sliced veggies or crackers.

Spicy White Bean Dip

Beans are a great way to increase your protein intake, and in this dip they are incredibly creamy! Enjoy it as a snack or on the side of a plate of salad to add some extra flavour and texture.

MAKES 1–2 CUPS

1 x 400 g can cannellini beans, drained and rinsed (or even better, 400 g fresh cannellini beans, cooked)
½ teaspoon curry powder
1 garlic clove, crushed

½–1 red chilli
2 teaspoons tamari
2 teaspoons sesame oil
1 tablespoon lime juice
3 tablespoons water

Place all the ingredients in a blender or food processor and process. Serve with chopped vegetables for dipping.

Quick Pickle

A quick pickle is different from a fermented pickle and won't have the same depth of flavour, but they are much quicker to make and get on your plate! Pick any vegetable, herb and/or spice you have on hand. Some of our favourite combinations are: carrot, coriander seed, garlic and ground turmeric; cucumber, mustard seed, dill and garlic; red onion with bay leaves; and carrot with black peppercorns, bay leaves, thyme and garlic.

MAKES 1 LARGE JAR

600 g vegetables, such as cucumbers, carrots, onions and green beans.
1–2 sprigs herbs, such as thyme, dill, rosemary and basil
2 teaspoons whole dried spices, such as mustard seeds, peppercorn and coriander seeds

2 cloves garlic, crushed
1 cup vinegar (white, apple cider or rice)
1 cup filtered water
1 tablespoon Celtic or Himalayan salt
1 tablespoon sugar (optional)

Clean a large jar with warm soapy water and dry completely.

Cut the vegetables into thin slices or your preferred shape or size.

Place them in the jar with the your choice of herbs and spices, packing them tightly.

Combine the garlic, vinegar, water, salt and sugar (if using) in a small saucepan over medium heat and bring to a simmer for a few minutes. Allow to cool slightly, then pour into the jar to completely cover the vegetables.

Tap the jar on the countertop a few times to allow all the water bubbles to escape. Seal with the lid and let the jar cool to room temperature, then refrigerate. Ideally wait at least 48 hours before trying the pickles, but you can eat them the same day if you wish. They will improve with age and will last in the fridge for up to 2 months.

Nourish Yourself

Kimchi

The art of fermenting food is deeply rooted in tradition, and has been a way of life for centuries throughout Asia. Eating fermented vegetables promotes the growth of healthy flora in the intestine because they are high in naturally occurring probiotics and enzymes. Gut health is not just important for digestive health, research shows it is also linked to autoimmune diseases, mental health, allergies and energy levels.

MAKES 3–4 JARS

½ green cabbage, finely shredded
   (you can also use white cabbage or
   a mixture of white and purple)
½ carrot, peeled and cut into matchsticks
¼ daikon or a handful of radishes, peeled
   and cut into matchsticks

2 tablespoons grated ginger
2–3 garlic cloves, minced
4 spring onions, sliced
2½ tablespoons salt
1 tablespoon gochujang (Korean chilli paste)
   or finely chopped red chilli.

Clean 3–4 jars with warm soapy water and dry completely.

Combine all the ingredients in a large bowl. Using your hands, massage the vegetables for about 10 minutes or until all of the juices have been released.

Pack the veggies tightly into the clean jars. Press the contents down into the jar so that the veggies are submerged under the liquid and most of the air bubbles are released. The juice should cover the veggies by about 1 cm. If you don't have enough juice to cover the veggies, add some filtered water. Wipe the rim and sides of the jars and seal.

Place the jars on a plate in a cool, dark, dry place for 7 days to allow the contents to ferment. The jars may start to bubble and some juice may escape.

After 7 days, store the kimchi in the fridge, where it will keep for up to 2 months.

Raw Sisterhood Golden Goodness Fermented Vegetables

Raw Sisterhood is a local Bondi company that makes the most amazing raw foods and fermented vegetables. This Golden Goodness recipe is their signature flavour and they have been kind enough to share it with us. Every time we make this recipe we remember Vivian, a close friend and one of the founders of Raw Sisterhood, who broke our hearts when she passed away – a true testament that our food can carry with it so much more than just flavour.

MAKES 2 LARGE JARS

2 green cabbages, finely sliced (save some
   of the outer layers for packing later)
6 carrots, peeled and grated
2 tablespoons grated ginger
1½ tablespoons crushed garlic

1 tablespoon grated turmeric (optional)
3 tablespoons ground turmeric
1 tablespoon caraway seeds
1 tablespoon fennel seeds
2 tablespoons salt, plus extra if needed

Clean 2 large jars with warm soapy water and dry completely.

Place all the ingredients in large bowl. Use your hands (you can wear rubber gloves to prevent your hands from getting stained by the turmeric) to mix and massage until the vegetables start to get soft and juicy. They should release quite a lot of juice – if not, just add some more salt. Spoon the mixture into the clean jars, packing them tight to leave out all air. Keep packing until the jar is full of veggies and the veggies are completely covered in juice – this is important. Leave some space at the top. Place a whole folded cabbage leaf on top to prevent any oxidation. Seal the jars with their lids.

During the fermentation process liquid will try to escape. We put our jars in a bowl and then a plastic bag to catch any juices that drip from the sides. Leave the jars to ferment at room temperature for 2–4 weeks.

When it's ready, it should be softly textured but not mushy, and have a fresh, spicy and acidic flavour. Discard the cabbage leaves at the top and store the jars in the fridge. They keep in the fridge for 6 weeks.

THREE

SWEET
SOMETHINGS

SWEET SOMETHINGS

What is the point of being healthy if you can't enjoy life? We make healthy choices to have energy and keep our bodies and minds operating in a state in which we can fully LIVE. One of the great joys in life is being able to enjoy the sweet stuff.

The key is for the sweets to be an enjoyment, not something we depend on for happiness or fall back on as an unconscious habit. And there are times, such as when we are doing a gut protocol or treating autoimmune issues through diet, that we steer clear of any sugars. But for the most part, when it comes to desserts, it is all about moderation.

And quality of ingredients. There is a big difference between the sweets you find in supermarket aisles (which can can resemble more of a science experiment than food) and the sweets you can make with REAL food. Nature provided us with a plethora of unprocessed sweetness; we just have to know what to do with it. The recipes in this chapter are decadent and luscious, and feature Asian-inspired tropical fruits and spices. They are perfect as a sweet treat just for you, or as a dessert to offer your friends when entertaining.

Pandan Panna Cotta with Miso Dressing

Pandan is a flavour that immediately transports you to Asia as it is extremely popular there. Look for it at your local Asian supermarket – it's the perfect complement to any dessert.

MAKES 12

1 × 400 ml can coconut cream
200 ml coconut water
3 teaspoons agar agar powder
1 teaspoon vanilla extract
3 tablespoons maple syrup
6 pandan leaves, tied in a knot to release
  extra flavour or 2 tablespoons homemade
  pandan essence (see note)
caramel miso, to serve (see page 175)

Combine the coconut cream, coconut water, agar agar, vanilla, maple syrup and pandan in a deep saucepan over low heat. Bring to the boil, then simmer gently for 10 minutes.

Pour the mixture evenly into ⅓ cup capacity moulds and place in the fridge to chill for 1 hour. (If you use deeper moulds the custard may split in the mould, giving the dessert a different texture.)

Turn the desserts out of the moulds onto serving plates and serve topped with caramel miso.

*Pandan Essence

Store-bought essence is full of artificial flavours. Instead, slice 20 pandan leaves, place them in a blender and cover with water. Blend for 3 minutes, then pour the liquid into a jar with a lid and refrigerate overnight. In the morning there will be two layers: light green at the top and dark at the bottom. Pour out the lighter top layer and use the darker layer as the essence.

Vanilla Black Rice Pudding with Roasted Plums

Black rice is a wonderful base for desserts, and has anti-inflammatory properties to lessen any guilt!
As with any cooked fruit, when you roast the plums they ooze sweetness and release their own syrup.
Nature's dessert, with no need to add artificial flavours or colours.

SERVES 4

½ cup black rice
1½ cups water, plus extra if needed
2 pandan leaves, tied in a loose knot (if you don't
    have these the dish is still tasty without them)
pinch of salt
1 vanilla pod, split and seeds scraped
    or 1 teaspoon vanilla extract
⅓ cup maple syrup
4 plums, halved, stones removed
1 cup coconut milk
2 tablespoons sesame seeds, lightly toasted

Preheat the oven to 180°C.

Place the rice and 1 cup of water in a medium saucepan, add the pandan leaves, salt and vanilla and bring to the boil. Reduce the heat and simmer for 25–35 minutes or until all the water has been absorbed and the rice is soft. You may need to top up the water during cooking.

Remove the pan from the heat, discard the pandan leaves and vanilla pod (if using) and stir in 2 tablespoons of maple syrup. Cover and set aside.

While the rice is simmering, place the halved plums, cut-side-up, in a baking dish and drizzle with the remaining maple syrup. Pour the remaining water into the dish, then place in the oven and roast for 20 minutes or until tender.

Pour the coconut milk into a amall saucepan and warm through for a few minutes.

Spoon the black rice into bowls and top each serve with 2 plum halves. Drizzle over the warmed coconut milk and finish with a sprinkling of sesame seeds.

Matcha Sago with Passionfruit Topping

Not your typical Western dessert, the matcha powder brings not only the flavour of green tea but also the benefit. Matcha contains a particularly potent class of antioxidant known as catechins, which are not found in other foods, and studies indicate they may have cancer-fighting properties.

Make sure you get a little passionfruit with each bite to add the sweet tanginess that complements the flavour of the matcha beautifully.

SERVES 6

Matcha Sago
1 cup sago (or you can use tapioca seeds)
2 cups water
2 cups coconut water
1 cup coconut milk
2 teaspoons matcha powder, or more to taste
pinch of salt
⅓ cup maple syrup

Passionfruit Topping
½ cup water
2 slices pineapple, finely diced
pulp of 10 passionfruit

To make the matcha sago, put the sago, water and coconut water in a deep saucepan and bring to the boil. Reduce the heat to low and simmer until the liquid has been absorbed and the sago is translucent.

Add the coconut milk, matcha powder, salt and maple syrup. Mix through and simmer for another 1–2 minutes, then set aside.

Spoon the sago into 6 small serving bowls or glasses, and place in the fridge for an hour to set and chill.

For the passionfruit topping, bring the water to the boil in a small saucepan, then reduce the heat to low. Add the pineapple and simmer for 4 minutes, then remove from the heat and set aside to cool.

To serve, spoon the pineapple over the sago puddings, top with the passionfruit pulp and serve.

* If you prefer a sweeter dish, top with a little chilled condensed coconut milk (see page 173).

Lychee and Peppermint Granita

Lychees are one of Asia's gifts to the world. There was a time when lychee martinis were our favourite pastime – this granita may not be as potent but it's just as tasty! The perfect end to a dinner party on a hot summer's night.

SERVES 4

1 × 565 g can lychees,
4 peppermint tea bags, steeped in 3 cups
  of boiling water for 5 minutes, cooled
1 tablespoon maple syrup
grated zest of 1 lime
1 × 400 ml can coconut cream – refrigerated for
  24 hours (Scoop off the firm coconut cream from
  the top and reserve the remainder for another use)

Place the lychees and syrup from the can into a blender and process until smooth. Strain and discard the solids.

Place the lychee puree and all the remaining ingredients in a large bowl and combine well.

Pour into a metal tray with sides , then freeze for 4 hours.

Scrape the granita with a fork to break it up, then serve immediately.

STRAWBERRY & ROSEWATER ICEPOLES
See page 158

BANANA & COCONUT ICEPOLES
See page 158

Strawberry and Rosewater Icepoles

We could dedicate an entire book to icepoles – they are so easy and fun to experiment with. Adding chia seeds boosts these little frozen sweets to give you a range of minerals, such as iron and zinc. There really is no reason to buy coloured icepoles when frozen fruits can taste this good.

MAKES 6–10, DEPENDING ON MOULDS

2 teaspoons chia seeds
500 g strawberries, hulled
3 tablespoons rosewater
2 tablespoons maple syrup

Soak the chia seeds in water for 5 minutes until they become gel-like in consistency.

Strain the chia seeds and add to a blender, along with the remaining ingredients and blend until smooth. Pour into popsicle moulds and freeze for 8 hours.

Banana and Coconut Icepoles

You can't go wrong with frozen bananas – they make any dessert sweet and creamy. Use over-ripe ones for the best-tasting results!

MAKES ABOUT 6, DEPENDING ON MOULDS

1 × 400 ml can coconut cream
5 frozen bananas, broken into chunks
2 tablespoons almond butter
1 teaspoon vanilla extract

Place all the ingredients in a blender and blend until smooth. Pour into popsicle moulds and freeze for 8 hours.

Coconut, Ginger and Lime Sorbet

This super light-tasting sorbet is heaven on a hot summers day!

20 g ginger, finely grated
1 × 400 g can coconut cream
1 × 400 g can coconut milk
3 tablespoons coconut sugar
1 teaspoon grated lime zest
juice of 1 lime
½ cup x toasted coconut flakes to serve (optional)

Combine all the ingredients in a large bowl, then place in the fridge to chill for 2–3 hours.

Transfer to an ice-cream machine and churn according to manufacturer's instructions. (If you don't have an ice-cream machine, pour the mixture into a shallow metal tray with sides and freeze until frozen and smooth, whisking every couple of hours.) Freeze for 4 hours or overnight before serving.

Raspberry Sorbet

This decadent sorbet is delightful for when you're having people over, especially served with some fresh berries on top.

1 cup water
½ cup raw sugar
4 cups fresh or frozen raspberries
juice of 1 lemon

Combine the water and sugar in a saucepan and bring to the boil, stirring until sugar has dissolved. Reduce the heat and simmer for 1–2 minutes, then remove from the heat and set aside to cool

Place the raspberries, lemon juice and sugar syrup in a food processor and blend until smooth. Pass through a sieve if you would like to remove the seeds. Chill in the fridge for 1–2 hours.

Transfer to an ice-cream machine and churn according to manufacturer's instructions. (If you don't have an ice-cream machine, pour the mixture into a shallow metal tray with sides and freeze until frozen and smooth, whisking every couple of hours.) Freeze for 4 hours or overnight before serving.

RASPBERRY SORBET
See page 159

COCONUT, GINGER AND LIME SORBET
See page 159

Caramelised Pears and Coconut Cream Parfait with Pistachios and Rosewater Fairy Floss

This recipe uses aquafaba, which is the brine in a can of chickpeas that we normally pour down the sink! Who knew it could be used as a binder similar to egg, or whipped up like cream? We know it sounds strange but trust us, it's worth trying! Using aquafaba will add a whole new dimension to your cooking and baking repertoire.

MAKES 6

5 ripe pears, peeled, cored and diced
juice of 1 lemon
100 g coconut sugar
1 tablespoon cornflour
1 heaped teaspoon ground cinnamon
aquafaba from 1 x 440 g can of chickpeas
  or white beans
1 teaspoon vanilla extract

pinch of cream of tartar
200 g coconut yoghurt, unsweetened
⅓ cup maple syrup
2 tablespoons pistachios, roasted
  and chopped coarsely
edible rose petals, to garnish (optional)
Persian fairy floss, to serve (optional)

Combine the pears, lemon juice and sugar in a medium saucepan and cook, stirring, over medium to high heat, until the sugar has dissolved and the mixture comes to a gentle boil. If the pears are not soft at this point, continue cooking for another 1–2 minutes until softened.

Add the cornflour and cinnamon and cook, stirring, for 1–2 minutes or until the mixture starts to thicken. Set aside to cool.

Using an electric mixer, whip the aquafaba, vanilla and cream of tartar on high until the mixture becomes light and fluffy. This could take anything from 4–10 minutes, depending on your machine.

In a separate large bowl, stir together the coconut yoghurt and maple syrup, then gently fold in the aquafaba mixture.

Layer the pears and yoghurt mixture in 6 small glasses or bowls – start with the pears and finish with the cream. Top with the pistachios, rose petals and fairy floss (if using).

Add the fairy floss just before serving so it doesn't melt into the cream.

Chocolate Coconut Slice

Whether you're a vegan or a meat lover, we believe everyone needs some chocolate in their lives. But you don't need dairy to get it and this amazing slice is testament to that.

MAKES 6–10 SLICES

1 cup shredded coconut, plus extra if needed
1 cup coconut flakes, plus extra if needed
⅓ cup sweetened condensed coconut milk
  (see page 173)
250 g dark chocolate, finely chopped

Line a 20 cm square baking tin with baking paper, allowing it to overhang the sides for easy removal of the slice.

Place the shredded and flaked coconut and sweetened condensed milk in a bowl and mix until combined. Press evenly into the prepared tin. If the mixture seems too wet, add a little more coconut.

Place the tin in the fridge to chill for 5 minutes.

Melt the chocolate in a heatproof bowl placed over a saucepan of simmering water, making sure the base of the bowl is not in contact with the water. Stir until smooth.

Pour the chocolate over the chilled coconut base and spread to cover evenly. Return to the fridge and chill until firm.

Once the chocolate is set, use the baking paper to remove the slice from the tin. Place it on a cutting board and cut it in half. Sandwich the halves together, coconut sides in, then cut into bite-sized pieces. Keep chilled.

Tahini Chocolate Fudge

Tahini should be a staple in every house. It's normally used for savoury dishes but it works wonderfully well in desserts too – epecially this one, making it as creamy and melt-in-your-mouth as any dairy fudge ever could!

MAKES ABOUT 10 PIECES

½ cup maple syrup
3 tablespoons coconut oil, melted
1½ cups hulled tahini
1 tablespoon raw cacao powder
2 teaspoons vanilla extract
2 teaspoons rosewater
3 tablespoons raw cacao nibs

Line a small tin baking tray with baking paper.

Place all the ingredients, except the cacao nibs, in a bowl and mix together well. Spoon into the prepared tray , smooth the top and sprinkle the nibs over the top. Place in the freezer for 4 hours or overnight.

Cut the fudge into bite-sized squares and serve as soon as you take them out of the freezer. They melt quickly!

Chocolate Chunk Brookies

Not a cookie, not a brownie, but definitely the best of both.

MAKES 12

½ cup almond butter
⅓ cup aquafaba (from a tin of chickpeas,
  white beans or black beans)
1 teaspoon vanilla extract
½ teaspoon bicarbonate of soda
¾ cup coconut sugar
⅓ cup cacao powder
70 g coarsely chopped dark chocolate
3 tablespoons chopped almonds or hazelnuts

Combine the almond butter, aquafaba and vanilla in a large bowl.

Place the bicarbonate of soda, sugar and cacao in a medium bowl and mix well.

Add the dry ingredients to the wet and stir to combine – the mixture will seem quite sticky. Add the chopped chocolate and nuts and gently fold through.

Refrigerate the brookie dough for 30 minutes.

Preheat the oven to 175°C. Line a large baking tray with baking paper.

Drop tablespoons of dough onto the prepared tray and press gently to flatten them slightly. Leave a little space between them to allow for spreading.

Bake for 9–12 minutes. After 9 minutes the cookies will be chewy and more along the lines of brookies. If you give them the full 12 minutes they will have a crisper texture and be more like biscuits. It's completely up to you!

Pistachio Kulfi

This melt-in-your-mouth dessert is so easy we guarantee you will be making it again and again! It's so creamy people won't believe it's not dairy.

MAKES 8

2 × 400 ml cans coconut cream
10 cardamom pods, bruised
½ cup raw sugar
1 teaspoon grated lime zest
50 g pistachios, roasted and chopped
ground cardamom, to serve (optional)

Place the coconut cream and cardamom pods in a saucepan. Bring to a simmer and cook gently over low heat for 15 minutes or until slightly thickened. Add the sugar and lime zest and stir until the sugar has dissolved.

Cool in the fridge for 1 hour, then strain and freeze for 30 minutes. Add ½ cup of pistachios and stir through.

Pour the mixture evenly into ½ cup-capacity moulds and freeze for 4–5 hours. Remove from the moulds and serve topped with the remaining pistachios and a sprinkling of ground cardamom (if using).

Sweetened Condensed Coconut Milk

You can actually make sweetened condensed milk out of any non-dairy milk. All you are really doing is reducing coconut milk to less than half the original amount, which can take some time. This is a good project to start if you are planning on being in the kitchen for a few hours and can keep a watchful eye on the stove.

MAKES ABOUT 1 CUP

650 ml coconut milk
½ cup coconut sugar
pinch of salt
½ teaspoon vanilla extract

Combine the coconut milk, sugar and salt in a medium saucepan over medium heat and bring to a simmer. Be careful not to heat the milk too much because it can burn and boil very quickly. When it reaches a simmer, reduce the heat to low and let it gently bubble away until reduced to about 1 cup.

Check the milk regularly to make sure it doesn't burn or boil over, stirring at regular intervals. The whole process can take up to 2 hours so stay close by. When the milk has reduced to the desired consistency, stir in the vanilla.

Serve the condensed milk hot or chilled.

Caramel Miso

This sweet sauce is heaven in your mouth. It's delicious drizzled over fruit, coconut ice-cream or panna cotta (see page 149).

MAKES HALF A CUP

½ cup coconut cream
3 tablespoons coconut sugar
1 teaspoon vanilla extract
1½ teaspoons miso paste (preferably white
  or yellow miso, but red is okay if you enjoy
  a stronger flavour)

Place the coconut cream and sugar in a medium saucepan over medium heat and bring to a simmer. Cook for 10 minutes or until reduced by half and the sauce is thicker and darker in colour. Make sure you whisk the cream constantly so it doesn't burn or crystallise in the pan.

Remove from the heat and leave to cool for 5 minutes, then whisk in the vanilla and miso.

Store the sauce in a sealed container in the fridge. It will keep for 3–5 days, but I doubt it will last that long – it tastes so good!

ACKNOWLEDGEMENTS

GEMMA

A massive shout out to Jody Pachniuk for his brilliant skills as a photography teacher, to James Joel for the tips, and for your helping hands, Tegan Haining.

Thanks also to Jess Gomes, who shared travels around Asia with me; Orchard Street for being a haven of wellness in Sydney and for creating the best juices around; and Raw Sisterhood for the veggies and the love you bring into this life.

Thank you to all the readers of my blog, The Compassionate Road, for helping to share the message that we can live healthy cruelty-free lives.

And of course so many thanks to Adam, Ariella and Jacob who let me turn our house into a commercial kitchen, food prop shop and studio for weeks at a time.

TRACY

I'd like to offer my thanks and gratitude to all of my family and friends for their ongoing support and encouragement.

Clint Paddison, thank you for showing me the true meaning of 'you are what you eat'.

To all the whole-food plant-based warriors out there, keep on keeping on!

And, lastly, the greatest thanks to those of you who have not only opened your homes, but also your hearts, and have given me the incredible opportunity to cook for you and your loved ones.

GEMMA DAVIS

Gemma is a naturopath, food photographer and mother. Her blog, The Compassionate Road, looks into health and food production. As a long-time supporter of Voiceless, the Animal Protection Institute, Gemma is acutely aware of the injustices and suffering that can occur on factory farms (where 80% of the world's meat now comes from) as well as the detrimental environmental impact this type of animal agriculture is having on our planet. Rather than dwelling on the problems, she is interested in the solutions and holds a deep curiosity around what drives people to make their choices – herself included.

I've spent many years working with people to help them overcome health issues through herbal medicine and supplementation but a HUGE part of living a healthy life, full of vital energy, comes down to nutritional education – what we do and don't put in our mouths, and of course the emotional triggers that influence *why* we put these things (or not) in our mouths. The food we choose to put on our table and our relationship with it is mammoth. We eat three times a day, every day!

Personally, I love food. I love time spent with friends, sharing meals. I don't want belief systems or health restrictions to ever get in the way of that, and they don't have to. Humans have come together to share food for eons. It is where we tell our stories, where our children and partners come together to download their days with us, along with their hopes and fears. It is where we can stop for a moment in our overly busy lives and nourish, laugh and reconnect.

Sometimes when we are learning new ways of eating there is a period of wobbles, which is completely normal for any change in life. Sometimes it is challenging to let go of habits that are not serving us – especially when they are rooted in our subconscious. Sometimes it is just plain tricky to find the time, especially as working parents, to cook wholesome meals the whole family will eat. Add to that trying new foods ... I hear you. I get it. But I also know it is worth it.

Having a basic understanding of nutrition and a playful attitude to cooking can change the way you experience life and the amount of energy you get to power you throughout your day.

As a parent I know it can change whole families. What our kids eat can literally change their behaviours and ability to learn and interact. It. Is. Worth. It.

Look at the ingredients lists on the back of food packets. Ask yourself, what is that ingredient? How was it made? How did it get to my plate? There is a story behind our food, and how it is produced affects more than just who is eating it.

The recipes in this book are plant-based but they are not just for vegans. Let go of the labels. We do not have to put ourselves in boxes and follow dogmas.

I don't want to harm animals or the environment, so I choose to eat plant-based food. I strongly believe that if more people knew the reality of factory farming, they too would not want to support the atrocities that occur in these places. I encourage you to learn more about the farming methods that have become standard practice in our society, for example see cowspiracy.com. If you eat meat, perhaps consider being a little more mindful by choosing to buy your meat from a different supplier, or eating a little less of it. That discussion is for another time, but it is important food for thought – pun totally intended.

This book presents you with delicious, healthy meals. Some of them may sneak in some sweetness, some of them combine melons with other foods (against food-combining law) and some of them contain gluten (shock horror). For the most part they are pretty damn healthy, and, since I am not a robot, I am 90% health conscious, but most definitely enjoy a little 'naughty' in my life too.

About the Authors

TRACY NOELLE

Tracy has been fortunate enough to combine all her passions into one role, traveling all over the world, learning, sharing, supporting and cooking in some of the most beautiful locations for beautiful people. She is grateful to have been invited into people's homes to help them transition into healthier lifestyles, to help them heal themselves physically and emotionally, and to facilitate a close, earthy connection to one another. She has cooked for celebrities, rock stars and prime ministers. She has cooked for those without homes, with life-threatening illnesses, and for families yearning to restore connection and intimacy within.

My real food journey began in my early 20s when I began to realise that microwave popcorn and beer was not going to sustain me in the long term. A good friend and foodie took pity on me and lent me a cook book which I experimented with. I was instantly hooked! I would yearn for the weekend when I could start an all-day cooking or baking project.

One day, I decided to take a leap of faith and quit my successful role in the tech industry to enrol in a culinary pastry course. I was so happy baking and eating sweet treats all day, every day! I also decided to eliminate meat from my diet after learning from several friends about the pain and misery most animals experience as part of our food-processing industry.

I started working full time in pastry kitchens across California but it wasn't until 10 years later that I made the connection between all the sugar, dairy and caffeine I was consuming and the tiredness and physical pain I was feeling every day. I went back to university to complete a Master's degree in Psychology and began working in mental health clinics in Sydney, where I began cooking lunches for my colleagues once a week. This led me to start a small catering company which kept me busy on the weekends and after work.

I loved cooking for families and small intimate gatherings. It brought back that grounding and connection I felt when I first started experimenting in my small apartment in San Francisco. During this time, I was introduced to some people who saw food in a very different way. They saw

food as a healing mechanism to prevent and cure disease and as a path to vibrancy and vitality. They challenged me to try a new way of eating to help me alleviate the allergies and seasonal hay fever that tormented me several times a year, as well as the constant tiredness, irritability and heartburn that seemed to follow me everywhere.

I was astonished how different I felt just by changing the type of food I consumed – not just physically, but emotionally too. After the first two weeks, my rosacea and heartburn disappeared, conditions I'd battled with prescription drugs for too many years! Within a month, my itchy eyes, puffy face and sniffly nose were gone. I couldn't believe what was happening! And my mood – I felt so calm and peaceful.

At last I made the connection between what I was putting in my body and how it was making me feel. After this discovery and transformation, there was no going back. I permanently changed the way I viewed food and, ultimately, my career!

With a strong culinary background as well as psychology and nutritional training, I was now well equipped to help others who were looking to change their eating habits – not just in the kitchen but by addressing the emotional connection as well ... which happens to be the strongest factor contributing to change and eating habits. Some believe that home is where the heart is. I now know that the heart is in every meal.

NOTES ABOUT OUR PANTRY

ASIAN-INSPIRED INGREDIENTS:

Pandan: Long dark green leaves that impart a unique vanilla, grassy fragrance to both sweet and savoury dishes. Available fresh, frozen or dried from Asian grocers, but fresh leaves will impart the most flavour.

Galangal: Often mistaken for ginger, galangal is common in Thai, Indonesian and Malaysian cooking where it is prized for its sharp earthy taste. Usually found near the ginger in supermarkets or Asian grocers.

Fried Shallots: Popular in South-east Asian dishes as a crunchy, flavoursome garnish. You can make your own, but store-bought ones are very convenient and readily available from supermarkets.

Matcha: Green tea powder made from green tea leaves. Matcha is very high in nutrients and energy boosting.

Mirin: A sweetened rice wine traditionally used in Japanese cooking.

Shichimi Togarasi: A Japanese spice mix which includes sansho (Japanese pepper), orange peel, red chilli pepper, garlic, sesame seeds, poppy seeds and nori. Used to flavour soups, curries and salads. It's a great mix to have on hand and we use it in many of our recipes.

BREADS:

Most breads today are hard for the body to digest and we're eating too much bread. Popular supermarket breads can be made with as many as 20 ingredients such as bleaching agents, plastic dough conditioners, preservatives, sugars, inflammatory oils and additives. These all help prolong shelf-life and compensate for the loss in taste due to faster processing times. Stay clear of these.

Good quality bread is made with minimal ingredients, takes longer to make and lasts for less time. Go for sourdough or sprouted breads, or try making your own seeded version. (We recommend The Life-Changing Loaf of Bread by My New Roots.)

RAW CACAO POWDER:

Made by cold-pressing the fermented and dried cacao beans which preserves the naturally occurring beneficial enzymes. Cocoa on the other hand, is made by roasting and processing the dried beans which reduces the nutritional value. We love using raw cacao in smoothies, hot chocolate and desserts.

CANNED FOODS:

If you're on a plant-based diet, attempt to get the most nutrients possible out of all your foods and when it comes to beans and legumes, there's no denying it's best to cook them yourself rather than using canned products. However, it's a reality of our busy lives that we sometimes need to lean on the can so just keep in mind that some food companies still line their cans with BPA which has been linked to health concerns. Look for cans which clearly state they are BPA free.

COCONUT OIL:

Don't be afraid of the high fat content – we love coconut oil and so do our hormones and moods! With a high-smoke point, coconut oil is a healthy alternative for cooking. It's also great in salads, baking or desserts.

DAIRY-FREE MILKS:

Almond, cashew, macadamia or coconut – really whatever nut you like can be made into a milk by soaking, then blending with water. It's so easy to make you'll be wondering why you didn't do it before. There are also pre-packaged nut and rice milks available but like every product, they vary in quality and ingredients. Look for the unsweetened ones with the least amount of ingredients.

Why not dairy? We are the only species that drinks a milk from another animal. This milk is designed to grow calves to 2000 kg. We're all for being healthy and strong but there's something about that equation that doesn't add up for achieving a healthy weight in human beings.

Lactase is the enzyme that is needed to break down lactose, however in humans we stop producing the enzyme at around 4-6 years old, which is a good indication that it is then hard for the body to digest. This may be why many people find dairy mucus-producing and the cause of common digestive symptoms such as cramps, diarrhoea and bloating.

There is also the issue of cruelty in the dairy industry. Female cows are continuously impregnated to keep producing milk and as a result, every new-born male calf is killed as "waste-product". The cows also are suffering in the now-common mega-dairies where they are kept confined and on concrete. Add the environmental pressures caused with their excrement, methane and water consumption when kept like this in mind-blowing numbers. It's nut milks all the way for us please.

EXTRA-VIRGIN OLIVE OIL:

Not all olive oil is the same! Make sure the oil you buy is cold-pressed (meaning heat has not been used in its extraction) as heat changes the compounds and can cause rancid acids to form. Never buy light or diet forms of olive oil, or in plastic containers, as they leach chemicals into the oils.

FRESH AND GROUND HERBS AND SPICES:

Packing a punch of flavour, nutrition and medicinal properties, some of the main spices we use in this book include:

Ginger: An anti-inflammatory, can bring pain relief and helps boosting digestive juices and neutralizing acids as well as decreasing intestinal contractions.

Turmeric: contains curcumin which studies show to be an excellent anti-inflammatory.

Cinnamon: improves blood sugar control, is an antibacterial and has anti-inflammatory properties, with studies showing it reduces pain linked to arthritis.

Coriander: is a digestive aid and is full of antioxidants.

Cumin: is a carminative (expels gas from the stomach and intestines) and digestive.

Parsley: has antiseptic and carminative properties and helps to stabilise blood sugar levels. Parsley tea relaxes stiff muscles and encourages digestion.

Mint: is a calmative and is incredibly soothing for the digestive system.

GLUTEN-FREE GRAINS:

Rices (black, wild, red, jasmine, basmati, sushi and brown), buckwheat, millet, quinoa and oats. Research and experience with clients shows that eating less or no gluten is helpful to feel more energised and reduce a host of health issues. This means swapping all or some of the wheat-based pastas and breads for grains such as these. But be aware that just because something is gluten-free does NOT mean it is healthy!

We have included some recipes in this book that include gluten-containing whole-grains because in small amounts, they also have their own benefits and can taste good, but if you have an issue with gluten, please just swap it out for one of the above.

GREEN SUPPLEMENT POWDER:

Add to your morning smoothie for a boost of vitamins and to help cleanse your system. There is a big range on the market, but we love Vital Greens, The Beauty Chef, Spirulina and Raw Super Greens.

KELP NOODLES:

Made from an algae seaweed, kelp noodles are high in iodine but don't taste like it! They're a great alternative to other noodles and when worked though in salads, they absorb the dressings like magic.

MISO PASTE:

A Japanese staple, miso is a salty, hearty paste, dense in nutrients and made from a fermentation of either soy, barley or rice or a combination of these. The different types or colours depend on which grain or legume was used and how long it was fermented for. We've used a variety of different miso pastes in the recipes, but if you only have one at home, just use that!

NUTS:

Ideally it's best to buy your nuts organic, raw and unsalted because pesticides can accumulate in them and when bought roasted they can contain rancid fats. It's easy to lightly roast and season raw nuts yourself, then eat them fresh from the oven. From a health perspective, it's also helpful to activate your nuts before eating to remove the phytic acid and enzyme inhibitors. These are naturally occurring in nuts and they bind to minerals in the digestive tract which makes it hard for us to absorb them. To activate nuts, soak the raw nuts overnight in filtered water, then bake them at around 65°C for 12-24 hours.

NUT SPREADS AND TAHINI:

Everyone should have these as pantry staples and we don't mean the commercial peanut butter. We're talking about almond butter, macadamia nut butter, cashew nut butter and tahini (sesame seed paste). These are found in most supermarkets in the spread or health food aisle. They're high in iron, zinc and protein and are great to have on crackers, in salad dressings, desserts or as dips. Make sure they contain no added sugar. Nut spreads are also easy to make yourself with a food processor!

ORGANIC OR NOT?

We prefer organic or pesticide-free where possible because it's better for the earth and the food has more nutrients and less pesticide residue. Soy products should always be organic. The Environmental Working Group publishes a useful list of the "Dirty Dozen" which is the produce that retains the most chemical residue that is also best consumed organic.

Do what you can. We shop at farmer's markets and get organic deliveries, then stock up during the week with other supplies. Life is about balance and making it work.

PROTEIN POWDERS:

Protein powders are not to be relied on but they can be a good way to supplement a diet when you use a good one that isn't full of artificial ingredients. We like natural flavoured fermented rice, pea or hemp ones the best.

SALT:

Standard table salt is refined and processed to the point that it is completely devoid of the naturally occurring nutrients. The quality of salt varies greatly depending on where it is mined and the level of refining that occurs – less being better! Himalayan, Celtic Sea, Maldon and Murray River salt are our favourites as they retain trace minerals such as magnesium, calcium and iron.

SESAME OIL:

Used in many of our recipes to add a nutty flavour. It's best to purchase the cold-pressed variety and store in the refrigerator.

SEAWEEDS:

(Nori, wakame, arame and dulse) Extremely nutritionally dense, seaweeds can be purchased in the Asian section of most supermarkets or in health food stores. They come dried and can either be crunched up and sprinkled over salads or soups, used to wrap sushi in, or cooked in water for hot dishes. Versatile and important to include in plant-based diets.

SEEDS:

(chia, flaxseeds, pumpkin, sesame, sunflower and hemp seeds) Keep jars of them in your cupboard. All of them. Seeds should be a pantry staple especially if you eat a plant-based diet as they are high in nutrients. Perfect as a quick snack, but also good to sprinkle on top of everything! Chia seeds can also be used in place of eggs in baking to bind, or soaked in water as puddings.

SPROUTS:

(alfalfa, snow pea sprouts, mung bean sprouts) Sprouting foods makes them more digestible because of the enzymes released. Whilst most sprouts are available from supermarkets, it's really easy to grow your own at home. Great in salads or as toppings on crackers and wraps.

SOY PRODUCTS:

Soy is a high protein food, popular for those on plant-based diets. What you want to aim for is that the majority of soy products you consume are organic and in the least processed form as possible. This means not making the "fake-meats" a staple in your diet, choosing products like tempeh (fermented soy beans), miso pastes or edamame instead.

SWEETENERS:

Maple Syrup: The sap from maple trees. High in thiamine, manganese and zinc, maple syrup has less fructose than honey, dates and agave. Make sure it's the real thing by checking the label, as the majority of "maple syrup" you find in the supermarket is actually artificially sweetened syrup which you want to avoid. Organic is ideal.

Rice Syrup: A little less sweet and more caramel in flavour than maple syrup and sticky in texture.

Coconut Sugar: High in minerals with a low glycaemic index, it can work as a substitute to brown sugar.

Sugar: While sugar can be rightly equated as the devil in the health-world because of the detrimental effects such as obesity and diabetes crisis, we still use it in some of our dessert recipes. The issue with refined sugar is how widely spread it is and that it is hidden in everything! Yet if you're going to indulge in a home-made dessert once a week that has a little sugar, we don't feel it is an issue. Less refined types of sugar are always a better choice.

Note in our opinion, aspartame is not a good alternative as a sweetener! It accounts for more reports of adverse reactions than all other foods and food additives combined.

TAMARI:

Similar to soy sauce but gluten-free and a little less salty. Made from the fermentation of miso.

VEGANAISE:

As the name suggests, a vegan version of mayonnaise. Used occasionally, it is great as it tastes wonderful. Found at health-food stores and supermarkets.

VEGETABLE STOCK:

Make sure you purchase vegetable stocks that don't have any artificial flavours or animal products by checking the ingredients.

WATER:

Filtered water is always the better option when you have the choice. While we are lucky to have access to fresh water from taps, it also contains some contaminants better to not have with every drink over a period of years. These can include nitrates from run-offs into our waterways from fertilisers in industrial farms, lead and aluminium from piping, chlorine (which acts as an antibacterial but it destroys Vitamin C, E, A and selenium in the body) and fluoride. While still controversial, there are some studies suggesting consuming fluoride can be harmful over the long term for some individuals. Avoid plastic bottled water as chemicals leach into the water and plastic bottles are one of the greatest contributors to the very serious problem of plastic waste in our oceans.

The Compassionate Kitchen: A Plant-based Cookbook
First published in Australia in 2018

A JULIE GIBBS BOOK
for

SIMON & SCHUSTER
AUSTRALIA
A CBS COMPANY

Simon & Schuster (Australia) Pty Limited
Suite 19A, Level 1, Building C, 450 Miller Street, Cammeray, NSW 2062
10 9 8 7 6 5 4 3 2 1

A CBS Company
Sydney New York London Toronto New Delhi
Visit our website at www.simonandschuster.com.au

 A catalogue record for this
book is available from the
National Library of Australia

Publisher: Julie Gibbs
Designer: Evi O. Studio
Food photography and styling: Gemma Davis
Lifestyle photography: Bayleigh Vedelago and James Joel
Home economist: Grace Campbell
Printed and bound in China by 1010 Printing International Ltd

The paper used to produce this book is a natural, recyclable product made from
wood grown in sustainable plantation forests. The manufacturing processes
conform to the environmental regulations in the country of origin.